GILLI DAVIES is a cookery writer and

In her native Wales she has written boo
food and she is a regular contributor to T

Her connections with Cyprus started i
husband, an army officer was stationed t

Her stay in Cyprus over a few years established a warm relationship with this beautiful island and its inhabitants, its good food, deeprooted customs and easy going life.

Through her enjoyment of Cyprus Cooking Gilli researched carefully into the culture and history of the island to produce this unique and exciting book.

While in Cyprus she contributed articles about Cyprus Cooking to the Cyprus Tourism Organisation, Cyprus Airways in-flight magazine Sunjet and to local radio and newspapers.

Interworld Publications Ltd.
12 The Fairway, New Barnet
Hertfordshire, EN5 1HN, England

First published in 1990
Re-print 1991

ISBN: 0 948853 13 1

Typeset in Century Schoolbook by
Sunset Typesetters

Designed and planned by Tophill Designs

Illustrations by Eddie Brockwell and
Renos Lavithis

Cover illustration by Eddie Brockwell

Colour Separations by L. Terry

Printed and bound in Cyprus by
PRINTO LTD, Nicosia

THE TASTE OF CYPRUS

A Seasonal look at Cypriot Cooking

by

GILLI DAVIES

Introduced by
George Michaelides

INTERWORLD PUBLICATIONS Ltd

I should like to dedicate this book to my husband Alun with whom I spent so many happy days discovering the flavours of Cyprus.

CONTENTS

ACKNOWLEDGEMENTS

An enormous thank you goes to all our Cypriot friends without whose help this book would never have been completed. In particular to Katerina and Tony Polycarpou who inspired and indulged us during our culinary discoveries and corrected my errors in the script.

Also to Eleftheria Pantazi of the Ministry of Agriculture and Natural Resources. Helen Stylianou, Renos Lavithis and the Cyprus Tourism Organisation who provided the photos. Many thanks also to the directors of Interworld Publications for their valuable assistance.

I hope with the book I will encourage visitors to Cyprus to stretch out and grasp the ever helpful hand of the Cypriot, to accept their warm hospitality and show a greater interest in the local cuisine.

INTRODUCTION

Once I was asked why we promote Cyprus as the island of the Gods when everybody knows that the Gods' home was Mount Olympus in Greece. With this I whole heartedly agree and I have no intention to disagree with the historians, but what is also true is that these same Gods used to come to Cyprus to spend their holidays and enjoy our local cuisine.

Today the island of the Gods presents itself as naked and beautiful as the goddess of Love, Aphrodite.

The leisurely pace of life on the island reflects the benevolent climate and revolves around agriculture, light industry, fishing, wine making and year-round tourism.

Food has always been as fascinating as the history of the island itself. Many civilisations have contributed to this living book of pictures taken from world history. First came the Greeks, then the Phoenicians, the Assyrians, the Egyptians, the Persians, the Romans, the Crusaders, the Francs, the Venetians, the Turks and the British — they all ruled Cyprus at one time or another and they all left their culinary secrets which blend harmonously in the Cypriot cuisine.

GEORGE MICHAELIDES
Marketing and Promotions Director, Louis Tourism
President of the European Federation

FOREWORD

"Within a week I had a dozen firm friends in the little town and began to understand the true meaning of the word - Kopiaste, which roughly speaking means 'Sit down with us and share'. Impossible to pass a cafe, to exchange a greeting with anyone eating or drinking without having the word fired at one as if from the mouth of a gun. It became dangerous even to shout 'Good appetite' as one does in Greece, to a group of labourers working on the roads when one passed them at their lunch hour seated under an olive-tree."

Lawrence Durrel in BITTER LEMONS

Welcome to Cyprus, Relax and let yourself slip into the Cypriot pace of life. As they say here ***siga siga*** slowly slowly. Feel the warmth of the climate and of the people, who will answer your every query with a cheery 'No Problem!' Take that seat by the sea, in the shade of a palm tree and sip your first **brandy sour.** Nibble on a nut or even better, pass the time with a handful of sunflower seeds or ***passa tempo*** as the Cypriots call them! As you idly split them between your teeth, let go, and enjoy your new found decadence.

Cypriots are a naturally hospitable race and generous to the extreme in a way that is so much part of the Middle East. In the Levant, as this eastern end of the Mediterranean is called, the inhabitants are of extremely mixed origin. Just a glance at the history of the Middle East shows how various empires, invasions, foreign settlers and traders have brought their influences to Cyprus. They also brought their recipes and many of these have been introduced into Cypriot cooking, the main ones coming from Greece, Turkey, Armenia, Lebanon and Syria.

These foreign flavours have combined with the food produced on the island to give Cyprus its own traditional cuisine.

A common factor to all Mediterranean countries is lack of fertile pastures, due to the arid climate. This limits the production of dairy produce and animals reared in the Levant are hardy lean beasts. The main crops are wheat, olives, vines, carobs and citrus fruits, but spices such as cumin, coriander, cinnamon and mastic have been grown for centuries and all these delicacies are exported from Cyprus to the Far East and Europe.

The Cypriots take pride in being self-sufficient and in rural areas they produce almost everything from pourgouri to cheese, bread and of course olive oil, nuts, grape juice products and even carob syrup.

Cypriots have an oriental love for very sweet things and their syrup soaked pastries are a delight to the eye but, alas, a threat to the waistline.

On the whole the Cypriot diet is healthy but frugal. For most families vegetarian meals make up the bulk of the diet with meat and fish being luxuries added here and there. What fine raw ingredients to start with though . . . fresh vegetables, nuts, herbs, pulses, vegetable oils, cheeses, yogurt and tons of fruit.

Just sniff Cyprus and you could become intoxicated by the tang of fresh lemons and the delicate citrus blossom, the wholesome smell of freshly baked bread or the fermenting grapes from the wine harvest.

Fast food in Cyprus might be a pitta filled with a kebab and salad, but slow food is more the order of the day. Food from the past too, such as figs, beans, chick peas, bitter herbs, olives, dates, almonds and nuts all of which are mentioned in the bible.

But the Levantine diet has come a long way since the Persian empire of c.500 BC introduced such high culinary standards, followed by the Greeks. Byzantium, the Eastern Roman Empire left its mark too. The Latins brought both French and Italian culture and diet to Cyprus before the dominance of the Ottoman Empire.

In more recent history, from the early part of this century after the collapse of the Ottoman Empire the Middle East has become cosmopolitan, crowded with people from all parts of the world who bring their diet with them.

Examples of recipes that arrived in Cyprus recently are the English Christmas cake, Italian pizza and the ubiquitous chipped potato, but also the Indian chapati which was adopted from visiting Indian troops stationed in Episkopi during the Second World War.

For the pastoral population of Cyprus, dependence on the natural elements is still great. Whether the weather brings drought, deluge, locust or earthquake, the farmers stand to lose their livelihood. The Cypriots are a God fearing people and the Greek Orthodox church is very strong, but this challenge against the elements brings a dependence on superstition, tradition and mystic culture.

The Orthodox calendar is dotted with religious fetes and saints days to satisfy the popular agricultural cults and there is a Saint for almost everything. For example, Saint Acoufos [St. James] prevents deafness, Saint Kyprianos drives away witchcraft and pains in the head, the protector of vines is St. Tychonas, while oxen come under the care of St Modestos, and the goddess Demeter looks after all crops.

Holy water is revered from sources island wide, each having its own healing properties. In many cases cures sought from a particular saint must be repaid to the incumbant with service or gifts to a particular monastery.

Another guarantee of a cure is to leave something behind. This can be seen to be an almost Homeric act, when he spoke of sacrifices near a spring under a plane tree with offerings from the faithful hung in the branches of trees. Pliny said that trees of all sorts were used as the first ancient temples. In his travel book, ***Slow boat to China*** Gavin Young describes how he found a tree hung with gifts on his trip across Cyprus.

There is still an idea that certain trees are holy and contact with them can curse or cure. Holy stones are revered too.

Visit any church and you will see wax models of childrens limbs; these ex-votos are offered to ensure that prayers for their well-being will be heard.

Cypriots have great respect for their Icons and the churches are adorned with a great many. The moving of these precious pictures is restricted to the priests.

The most famous of all Cypriot goddess' is Aphrodite who according to history came to Cyprus from the Phoenician mainland. Her true genealogy must go back to the Phoenician queens of heaven, of love and fertility, to mother-goddesses of Assyria, Babylon and Sumeria which suggests to us that she was the Phoenician goddess Astarte.

Tradition says that she stepped ashore at a point on the south west coast of the island at Petra tou Romiou, not far from her temple city of Old Paphos, where a peculiarly thick and creamy foam boils up and surges on to a shelving beach, under pink rocks and cliffs. There she founded her immortal kingdom and all the gods wished to marry her.

Another local legend says that Aphrodite used to bathe herself in a spring in the Akamas, at the western end of Cyprus overlooking Khrysokhou Bay.

Aphrodite has brought such romantic connotions to Cyprus that Euripides wrote in his play The Bacchae

"O to visit Cyprus,
Aphrodite's island,
Where her Erotes
Dwell, who stroke
Their spell on
Mortal men . . .

Mortal men of every kind are drawn to Cyprus, archaeologists, romantics, travellers, gourmets, naturalists and holiday-makers. I hope that this book brings to them a feeling of warmth, not only from the Cyprus sunshine but also from the charm of the Cypriot people.

When preparing recipes from the book, think yourself into a Cypriot kitchen, surrounded by simple, fresh ingredients. Remember too the importance that every Cypriot places on preparing and presenting food.

"Fasting and sharing food with guests and strangers is a matter of honour and a ritual. Food is not only a source of nourishment but a focus for socialising and entertainment".

Lawrence Durrell in BITTER LEMONS.

THE TASTE OF CYPRUS

Cypriots are proud to be self sufficient.

Most families own at least a little piece of land and on it they will tend and care for perhaps a lemon, orange or tangerine tree, fresh herbs of all kinds, an olive or carob tree, probably an almond tree or walnut tree and as many vegetables as they have room to grow.

Visit a traditional Cypriot housewife at any time during the year and find her busy with seasonal produce. Whether its picking vegetables for the winter or dropping summer fruits into heavy syrup. Distilling the essence from the bitter orange flowers in the spring or boiling up grape juice in the autumn to make sweets for the children.

Situated as it is, right at the heart of the Levant, Cyprus has benefitted from a variety of Middle Eastern cuisines as well as Greek over the centuries. One of the more fascinating aspects of cooking Cyprus dishes is to delve into their origin, trying to decipher from where, how and when they arrived on the island.

Take houmous for instance, a very Lebanese dish. Did this arrive recently with the many Lebanese who have sought peace in Cyprus since the troubles in their home country or did houmous come to Cyprus over two centuries ago when due to persecution during the Ottoman rule, so many Cypriots fled to Lebanon, only to return when the climate in Cyprus became calmer.

Baklava, that sticky sweet pastry layered with nuts and honey has a confused past. It bears a very close resemblance to so many of the pastries that are so much part of the Turkish cuisine. The name Baklava smacks of a Turkish or Arab past, yet, according to Rena Salaman, it has its roots in ancient Greece as it is clearly described by the Greek author Athinaeos in the second century AD.

In Cyprus, puddings can be creamy, sweet and aromatic or rich pastries that fill the bakery shelves. They are generally eaten during the day rather than at the end of a meal, when fruit is normally offered.

What are the main flavours of Cyprus then?

Olive oil and fresh lemon juice season most dishes and appear to be more vital to the dining table than salt and pepper. For instance, a dish of hot vegetables are transformed into a warm salad by a quick dosing in olive oil and lemon juice.

Parsley, mint, fresh coriander, basil and wild marjoram are the favourite herbs with cinnamon by far the most popular spice.

Fresh fruit and vegetables are the mainstay of the diet with pulses and pulse based dips playing an important part. They love nuts and have a real fondness for sweet things too.

Meat and fish are not eaten every day at home, but always when a Cypriot eats out.

Cypriots generally eat a healthy diet.

They breakfast on olives, bread and a slice of halloumi cheese though during the summer months water melon makes a major addition.

Lunch is usually the main meal consisting of maybe fish or a meat casserole with pulses and some fresh vegetables.

For the evening meal, bread, cheese and salad suffice.

Some of the tips I have gleaned from Cypriot cooks seem so sensible and easy I shall never forget them.

Grating fresh tomatoes straight into a dish makes sense and cuts out a lot of tiresome pealing and slicing.

Almonds are more often than not used with their skins on. The flavour seems to be improved and they are certainly more moist.

Olive bread, if you like olives, is the most marvellous meal on its own. Succulent and full of flavour, who needs more?

Pourgouri or cracked wheat is one of the easiest and most nourishing ingredients to use. Whether you make a pilaf, a salad or stuff the turkey with it.

Cooking vegetables like cauliflower and potatoes in a little red wine and crushed coriander seeds — magic!

Adding a little olive oil to cooked pulses gives them a richness they deserve.

Throwing a handful of fresh herbs on the grill as you barbecue to tantalize the tastebuds of hungry anticipators.

And perhaps lastly, the use of fresh lemon. Whether it is squeezed into a kebab filled pitta or over a pork chop, in a honey syrup for pastries or into a refreshing drink, it is quite indispensable.

CYPRIOT COOKING TIPS

"If the stone falls on the egg, alas for the egg
If the egg falls on the stone — alas for the egg"
Greek Proverb

To use this book you must adjust a little and learn to cook like a Cypriot. Cypriots cook with a smile, a shrug, lots of patience and more than a little tasting! One of the most important words to apply to Cypriot cooking is ***PERIPOU*** which means approximately!

After all, does it really matter that the carrots are bigger than expected or the courgettes rather small. Add a spoonful of oil, or two, and perhaps a little more lemon juice.

Modern cookery influences came slowly to Cyprus, and Cypriots on the whole, still learn to cook from their mother. Only a small percentage own a food processor, something I find indispensable when preparing Cypriot dishes.

Remarkably few cooks in Cyprus possess a pair of scales. The all important measure is the glass. It is used universally throughout domestic kitchens and even pastry is cut using the rim of the glass in a wheel movement.

What size glass, I hear you ask? — Not a very big glass, just a smallish tumbler, the most important factor of every recipe being that you must use the same glass throughout.

I have, in all recipes given both glass and imperial measurements, but I hope that you will try the **GLASS** method of measuring. It may be rather strange to leave the scales in the cupboard and reach for the drinks cabinet . . . but once you have succeeded with one or two recipes I think you may never want to return to pounds and ounces or kilos and grams. Trust, have faith, and find the right size glass!

1 glass = 200ml or 7 fl. oz.

INGREDIENTS FOUND IN A CYPRIOT KITCHEN

ANARI - fresh goat and ewe's milk cheese similar to ricotta. Eaten with honey and spice or salted and left to dry till hard and grated like parmesan

ARTICHAT - cumin, a vital ingredient in the Cypriot dish tavas.

BAMIES - okra or ladies fingers.

BAKALIAROS - dried salt cod, a favourite winter ingredient.

CHAIMAN - fenugreek, a bitter herb that is used in spiced Pastourma.

CHINOS - juniper, used in Loukanika sausages and a flavouring for cured pork.

ELIÉS - olives, which have been enjoyed as a fruit and for their oil from ancient times.

FAKÉS - lentils, either green or brown and the small red variety are all available and much used.

FÉTA - A soft, crumbly Greek cheese made from goat's or ewes milk. Stored in whey.

GARÍFALA - cloves, sometimes used to spice tea, and often included in both sweet and savoury dishes.

GLYSTIRIDA - purslane, a salad ingredient with green fleshy leaves.

HALVA - literally means sweet and is generally associated with the confection from ground raw sesame seeds, which sometimes contains almonds or pistachio nuts.

HALLOUMI - A ewes, goats and cows milk cheese made from whole milk which is stored in whey and has a rubbery texture. It is good when grilled or fried. Halloumi may be flavoured with mint.

KANELLA - cinnamon, a popular spice for both savoury and sweet dishes, sold powdered or as pieces of bark.

KEFALOTIRI - a full fat hard cheese made from ewe's and goats milk with the addition of cows milk sometimes. It is matured for 6 months.

KOUKIA - broad beans, sold fresh in the summer and dried in the winter.

KOLIANDROS - coriander, sold fresh as a pungent leaf similar to parsley, or in seed form which has a faint orange flavour.

KOLOKASSI - a species of taro that comes from the Pacific Islands. Rather like a sweet potato.

LOUVI MAVROMATI - Black-eyed beans.

MAHLEPI or MAHLAB - A Syrian spice from the kernel of the black cherry stone, with a sweet spicy fragrance. The spice is always sold whole and is a small husked seed, pale brown in colour and a little smaller than a coriander seed. Pound in a mortar before using to flavour sweet yeast breads. A reasonable alternative is allspice.

MASTIC - mistik in Arabic. It is a resin from a small evergreen tree with most of the world's supply coming from the Greek island of Chios. Cyprus is now producing mastic in the Paphos region. From ancient times it has been used as a chewing gum. The powdered resin is used to flavour sweet yeast breads and a Greek liqueur of the same name. In Egypt a small piece of mastic is often added to boiling chicken to remove unwanted flavours. Over a century ago — the scale of a single ounce was punishable by death. Mastic was indispensable to the ladies of the Sultan's household, the ladies prized it highly for their teeth and the gentlemen were fond of chewing it.

MARATHO - fennel, the wild variety is much loved by the Cypriots who gather it in armfuls in the spring.

MAVRO KOKOS - Known as black cumin, it is used on sweet yeast breads and cakes in Cyprus, Lebanon, Syria and Armenia.

METANO - flat leaf parsley — the most commonly used herb in Cyprus.

NEROLI - orange flower water is used as a flavouring or in a syrup for most sweet pastries.

PASTOURMA - Dried, highly spiced beef and sausages.

POMEGRANATE (Rovi) - trees grow everywhere in Cyprus. Originating, perhaps in Persia where the juice is used in so many recipes. On the whole the Cypriots eat pomegranates just as they are, scooping out the pearly pink seeds with a spoon. There is however a dish called **Golliva,** incorporating almonds, cooked whole wheat, currants, cinnamon and pomegranates and is prepared to commemorate the death of a relative.

POURGOURI - burghul, bulgar or cracked wheat. Hulled wheat, steamed until partly cooked, dried then ground. Available in fine and coarse grades.

RESSI - is the traditional dish served at weddings. It is made from wheat which is cooked over a long period with lamb and a large amount of lamb fat. It is very rich and a good ressi is a real delicacy.

REVITHIA - chick peas, sold whole or split.

RIGANI - Cyprus wild marjoram or oregano. The name origanum comes from Greek meaning 'joy of the mountains' which is very suitable because it grows like a weed all over the Troodos mountains in Cyprus.

SESAME - sesame seeds used as a flavour for baking and tahini dip.

SKORTHO - garlic.

TAHINI - an oily paste made from toasted sesame seeds.

THENDROLIVANO - rosemary.

THIOSMIS - mint, used throughout Cypriot cuisine.

TRAHANAS - small biscuits of dried wheat and yogurt used to flavour nourishing winter soups.

YOGURT - The Turks lay claim to the discovery of yogurt, and it is first mentioned in Turkic Buddhist texts of the eighth century. The story tells how Turkish bedouins carrying provisions over the saddle found one day that the heat and continuous movement had turned their milk supply to yogurt. Yogurt is served with almost every meal in Cyprus and although in most of the countries of the Middle East yogurt is used in cooking, in Cyprus as in Greece, cold yogurt is served separately. Its sharp acidity brings a freshess to the mouth with such an oil rich diet.

100
80

15
30
25

Index to Category of Recipes

Fish (contd.)

Spring

The spring sunshine is welcome when it arrives after the winter rains and colder weather, and Cyprus turns green.

Green, green, green. In spring Cyprus goes through a metamorphosis, as the parched land becomes fertile and yields lush crops.

During these cooler months in Cyprus a wealth of edible green vegetables appear on the market stalls. The Cypriots prepare them in a variety of ways; either wrapping their greens in delicate filo pastry to make pies or pittes, tossing them into omelettes or simply boiling in water then dressing with olive oil and fresh lemon juice just before serving.

Look out for bundles of huge leafy **artichokes,** choose the purple tipped ones for the best flavour. They are sold with long stems and are often served sliced and raw, in fact the whole artichoke tastes delicious when raw and is considered quite a luxury served this way.

Spinach comes in large and small leaf varieties with a larger brother in the shape of juicy green **lahana** or chard. These can be cooked in the same way as spinach or used as the wrapper for a variety of fillings, like vine leaves.

Fresh herbs and salad stuff are available such as **leaf coriander, glystirida** or purslane, **rocket** and **dandelion leaves.** One of the more unusual greens is **louvana,** a type of vetch or pea plant, the curly tendrils are easy to recognize and the flavour adds a pleasant sharpness to your spring diet. Fresh peas and broad beans so young and tender that they are simply stripped down the sides and cut through, pod and all before being lightly boiled and then dressed with the ubiquitous Cypriot dressing of olive oil and fresh lemon juice.

Have you eaten **kohlrabi** the Cypriot way, finely sliced and dressed with pure lemon juice, freshly squeezed and a good sprinkle of salt?

Spring onions so large as to be mistaken for leeks, pungent wild garlic and the feathery tops of **maratho** wild fennel, sweet and delicious. Don't miss the wild asparagus **agrelia** either, when it appears during March. Take care with its cooking though, don't plunge it into boiling water and wait until the stems are tender, for the heads will have fallen off long ago and the flavour will be mostly in the water! Cook it as the Cypriots do, simply cut off the woody part of the stem and toss the heads gently in oil or butter. Serve straight from the pan.

Talking of wild things, just watch the indigenous population of Cyprus enjoy their greens picked from open pastures, wayside scrubland and even the roadsides. Don't be surprised if the car in front of you stops suddenly and the occupants dive for the hedge, only to re-emerge with handfuls of weeds, and these are not to be taken home for the domestic rabbit!

They will be gathering **moloshes** or mallow plants, **strouthouthkia** or cow parsley, and **mangalli** which is an edible type of thistle.

Herbal lore is still practised in Cyprus. Moloshes were well known to the ancient Greeks, and are prepared as an infusion for internal gastric problems. Children rub them on to stinging nettle rashes too.

Fennel is used as a tonic, digestive and expectorant. It is prepared either as an infusion or a tincture, and wild asparagus, wild garlic and dandelion leaves are good for you too as is of course the illustrious olive.

Spring in Cyprus is fresh and very special. Enjoy it as the Cypriots do. Pack some bread and wine, leave your worries at home and head for pastures green, *and* most important, don't forget to take some baskets with you!

CARNIVAL FOLLOWED BY LENT

Of all the periods of fasting during the Greek Orthodox Calendar, and there are a great many, none is taken more seriously than Lent.

During Lent devout Cypriots eat nothing derived from an animal, fish or fowl, but most endure a seven week ordeal of fasting and prayers in order to achieve spiritual perfection. To prepare the body for these frugal times Lent is preceded by ten days of fun and feasting in the period known as *Carnival.*

There is a Cypriot proverb which says "At Carnival time even the dogs overeat".

Carnival begins on a Thursday, which the Cypriots call 'Tsiknopefti' or smelly Thursday (Tsikna comes from the classical **knisa,** which mean the smell of cooking). On Tsiknopefti and the days which follow, everyone grills meat. Visit any town or village in Cyprus and you will see smoke rising from the most basic of grills, often placed in the street for lack of space anywhere else, wafting delicious smells of grilled meats into the air.

Everyone loves Carnival! Families gather eagerly to prepare their fancy dress and arrange parties. In Limassol on the south of the Island huge processions wind through the streets, floats laden with colourful characters. Music streams out of every doorway and open window and girls of all ages dance their way in and out of the procession.

Ravioli *and filo pastry* **bourekia** filled with spiced meat are the specialities of the first week of the carnival. Also there are delicious **daktyla** or ladies fingers which are crisp pastries filled with chopped almonds and spices, and **kateyfi,** sticky cakes made from a mesh of pastry strands which are soaked in rose-water syrup.

Carnival ends on Tyrofagos or cheese eating Sunday and the ravioli and bourekia change their filling to halloumi cheese with mint. Halloumi, native to Cyprus is made from goat or sheep milk. It has a slightly rubbery texture and cooks well.

Carnival closes with the biggest and best parades and largest feasts of all. Friends and neighbours are encouraged to join in the family feast because the tables must be cleared of all rich and feasting foods in preparation for Lent the following day.

The first day of Lent is called Clean Monday. After an early rise the Cypriots wash their houses from top to bottom. Then, after a cursory glance at the sky to check that sunshine is in order, they make for the fields with a picnic. Baskets full of fresh vegetables, olives, oranges and bottles of wine.

It sounds a fine healthy diet and to many this Lenten fast is most appealing. Pulse dishes of every kind appear on the menu. **Fasoulia** is one of the favourites, a casserole of haricot beans, cooked till tender then served with a dressing of olive oil and lemon juice. Pourgouri, burghul or cracked wheat mixed with vermicelli and cooked with oil makes a delicious nutty pilaf, always served with yogurt. Greens such as spinach or chard taste delicious when cooked with black eyed beans and make a good filling meal **louvia me lahana.** At this time of year the markets in Cyprus are simply brimming over with fresh vegetables, all grown locally.

Citrus fruits are in season during these early months of the year. Oranges, tangerines, grapefruit and clementines fill the roadside stalls. Their high vitamin content must help to keep the fasting population fit!

Olives add healthy goodness to the Lenten diet. Full of oil they add a richness to most meals. Olive bread or **eliopitta** is delicious and makes a meal in itself, but be warned, many an unsuspecting visitor has broken a tooth on a hidden stone!

Other Lenten pastries are **spanokopittes,** made from layers of delicate filo pastry with a filling of spinach, while **tahinopittes** are doughy pastries with a layer of sweetened tahini paste spread through the middle. Perhaps the most unusual pitte to look out for during Lent is the **kolokopitta.** Inside this pastry is a filling of cooked red pumpkin, cracked wheat and raisins . . . a very good mixture of flavours . . . !!

St. Lazarus' day falls on the Saturday before Holy week. St. Lazarus is considered to be a very special saint in Cyprus for it is said that after his resurrection by Christ he lived and died in Cyprus, at Kitium. He is the Patron Saint of Larnaca and a big church there bears his name. In his honour people make necklaces with wild gladioli and yellow daisies which grow in great profusion at Easter time in the fields of Cyprus. The next day, Palm Sunday the children put on their Sunday best and gather olive branches or palm leaves to take to church to welcome Christ who made his entry into Jerusalem on this day.

Easter week arrives and Cyprus literally glows in its new spring colours with wild flowers in bloom everywhere. **Lambri** is the name given to the Feast of Easter. It means 'shining' literally the Feast of Light. As in all parts of the Christian world the egg plays an important part in the Easter celebration, being the giver of life, and in Cyprus eggs are cracked together at Easter by children and adults alike. During Holy Week children delight in dyeing their eggs red with a root called rizari which is sold in the markets.

During this final week of Lent people go to church in the morning and evening and the fast becomes harder, even olive oil is forbidden. But the end is in sight and every housewife equips herself to make the most traditional Easter speciality of all, **flaounes.** Combining all the things forbidden during Lent, these rich pastries filled with cheese, eggs and flavourings take two days to prepare. The recipe differs from region to region, and family to family, some flaounes are sweet with raisins, some contain mint and the shape can differ too, but common to all flaounes is the special cheese prepared only at this time of year. On sale for such a limited period, this fresh lightly pressed cheese made from ewe and goat milk sells at a premium. Everyone buys flaouna cheeses, which get their tall cylindrical shape from the dalari or reed baskets in which they are made.

The 'cheesecake' type filling, combining grated cheese, eggs, yeast, mint and seasonings is prepared on the evening of Thursday during Holy Week, and the baking of the flaounas takes place on Good Friday. Unless you have an old outdoor beehive oven it is wiser to send your flaounas to the local bakery where they will take their turn to be baked.

Here is a fine Cypriot saying which goes "On Good Friday one avoids housework lest the house gets infested with crickets", so instead the morning is devoted to the decoration of the Holy Sepulchre in Church with a mass of fresh flowers.

At lunchtime the traditional **"Faki Xidati"** vinegar and lentil soup is eaten, containing vinegar because it is said that when Christ asked for water on his way to Calvary He was given vinegar instead.

In some regions of Cyprus they make the bread of May, a sort of cake in the centre of which is put a red egg and a cross. It is hung on the wall or door of the house and won't be taken down till the first of May, on which date it will be eaten to protect the inmates against being bitten by donkeys — or so they say!

At last it is Easter Weekend and families gather together for the main celebration of the year. Known as 'free weekend', children return home knowing that they will be received joyously and generously by their parents.

During Saturday the youngsters gather fire wood which they pile up in the churchyard and in the evening the bonfire is lit to signify the burning of Judas.

Saturday night and everyone goes to church. The air is alive with excitement and as soon as the priest declares "Christ is risen", the air rips with joy and the fast is broken.

Families returning home will crack eggs and then settle down to a nourishing bowl of **avgolemoni soup** before making for bed.

On Easter day throughout Cyprus they eat **souvla.** Large chunks of lamb threaded onto skewers and grilled, served with potatoes and salad. After the stringency of Lent just watch the Cypriots relax! They sing, dance, break eggs with each other and turn the Easter lamb on the spit. A sunshine celebration as if there is no tomorrow.

KAFÉS — CYPRUS COFFEE

Whatever your errand in Cyprus it is almost impossible to visit the shops or market without being offered a coffee. Such is the charm and warm hospitality of the Cypriot race.

"Relax, what's the hurry anyway, surely you have time for a coffee!" A nescafe or **nes** will be offered to any visitor but perhaps you would prefer some of the real thing.

Cypriots drink Turkish coffee, although since the troubles of 1974 it is known more often as Cyprus coffee (or Greek coffee).

It is made individually in small long handled pots, wide at the base and tapering in at the top. These are called **Imbrikia** and come in various sizes, from individual to a many cup size.

Fresh coffee beans, usually Brazilian, are finely ground or powdered daily and one heaped teaspoon is added to each demitasse of cold water. Sugar goes in too at this stage before heating the coffee. You need to know whether to order *glykos* (sweet) *metrios* (medium sweet) or *sketos* (unsweetened).

The imbrikia are heated on the stove and when the sugar has dissolved the coffee is allowed to come to the boil, forming a creamy froth on top called *kaimaki*. As the froth turns in from the sides and the coffee begins to rise in the pot, it is removed from the heat and poured, a little into each cup, to distribute the froth.

Cyprus coffee is strong and should always be served with a glass of cold water. It contains no spices, such as the cardamom pod you might find in a cup of Arabic coffee, but sip with care, for at the bottom of every cup lurks more than a little sediment!

• Anginares — Globe Artichokes •

There is a legend from the Aegean island of Zinari about a beautiful girl called Cynara who lived there. She was so beautiful that a jealous goddess turned her into a globe artichoke, and her name lives on in the Greek word Anginares.

Artichokes are a real favourite in Cyprus. Their leafy heads fill stalls in the market from November until well after Easter, and although the early green variety is good the later purple one is worth waiting for.

Artichokes are eaten quite raw by the Cypriots — *Anginares Omes*. Simply cut into quarters, with the choke removed and served with a good squeeze of lemon. They have a pleasant flavour and a remarkable aftertaste, which leaves you reaching for a drink. The perfect appetizer.

The French eat their artichokes plain boiled with vinaigrette or hollandaise sauce while throughout the Middle East and Greece there are a variety of ways combining artichokes with other vegetables or different sauces.

This recipe calls for the hearts of the artichokes only, but I cook the leaves too and serve them with a hollandaise sauce for the family to dip into.

If you are in doubt about this recipe try it first with tinned artichokes hearts and frozen beans. You'll be a convert in no time.

• Serves 6 •

Ingredients

6 fresh artichokes
juice of 2 lemons
3 tablespoons olive oil
2 cloves garlic, crushed with salt
pinch of granulated sugar
1½lb (700g) fresh broad beans, shelled
1 tablespoon chopped parsley or rigani
black pepper
1 tablespoon cornflour mixed (slaked) with 1 tablespoon water

1. Bring a large pan of water to the boil and let the artichokes simmer for about 5 minutes. Then rinse under the cold tap. They should be easier to prepare like this.

Peel off the leaves (throw them back into the pan for another 5 minutes if you want to eat them by themselves) and scrape out the choke or thistle like centre. Trim the stem from the base of the artichoke heart.

2. Put the hearts into a large pan with the lemon juice, oil, garlic, sugar and about 1 glass/200ml water. Bring to the boil and add the shelled beans, herbs and pepper. Turn down the heat and simmer for between 30-40 minutes, until the vegetables are tender and the juices much reduced.

3. Lift the artichoke hearts and beans out of the pan and add the slaked conflour to the juice, stirring all the time. Boil until the sauce thickens and clears. Pour the sauce over the vegetables and serve hot, warm or cold.

• Avgolemono—Egg and Lemon Soup •

This delicious Greek soup is made all over the Eastern Mediterranean. In Cyprus it is traditionally served on Easter Morning to break the long lenten fast.

Avgolemono, with its clever combination of egg and lemon has a rather pleasant, slightly tart flavour. This simple combination appears in many suaces as well as fish and vegetable soups.

If you have a pot of stock on the go, then here is the perfect instant soup for you.

• Serves 6 •

Ingredients

2 pints well flavoured chicken stock

2 oz (50g) rice

salt and pepper

2 eggs

juice of 1-2 lemons

2 tablespoons finely chopped parsley or chives (optional)

1. In a large saucepan bring the chicken stock to the boil.

2. Add the rice and simmer until cooked. Take the pan off the heat and allow the soup to cool a little.

3. Beat the eggs and lemon juice together in a bowl. Add a spoonful of the warm soup, stir well and blend the egg mixture back into the soup, stirring all the time. Reheat the soup carefully, taking care not to let it boil, or it will curdle.

4. Taste for seasoning. Don't be afraid to add salt, it will only improve the lemon flavour rather than drown it.

5. Serve the soup immediately, garnished with chopped parsley.

• Khorta Sto Fourno — Oven Baked Vegetables •

For the majority of Cypriot families, vegetables and pulses make up the basis of every day meals. Meat and fish still being fairly special ingredients, eaten two or three times a week.

This recipe is typical of a family meal, cheap and tasty, and ideal for the many weeks of the year when the Greek Orthodox faithful are fasting.

• Serves 4-6 •

Ingredients

2 tablespoons olive oil
1 medium onion, sliced
2 cloves garlic, crushed
2oz (50g) stoned black olives
2 large firm tomatoes grated - or 1 425g can of tomatoes, well mashed
1 tablespoon tomato puree dissolved in a glass of hot water
a handful of chopped parsley
2 large potatoes, peeled or scrubbed and sliced thinly lengthways
2 medium courgettes, sliced lengthways
1 medium aubergine, sliced lengthways
1 green pepper, sliced into rings
1 teaspoon rigani, oregano or marjoram
4oz (100g) tasty cheese, grated
salt and pepper

1. Heat the oil in a saucepan and cook the garlic and onion until soft but not brown. Add the olives, tomatoes, tomato paste and parsley. Season and simmer for 10 minutes.

2. Oil a large casserole dish and layer the potatoes, courgettes and aubergines in the bottom. Sprinkle over half of the cheese. Add the green pepper and oregano.

3. Pour over the tomato sauce and cover with the remaining cheese.

4. Bake the vegetables, uncovered, in a medium oven gas 4, 350°F, 180°C for between 45 mins to an hour, depending on the depth of the dish.

• Cauliflower Afelia Style•

Lula, a friend from Paphos, who is a superb cook gave me this recipe. Think of the British cauliflower cheese — so comforting for a cold winters day, and compare this wine and spice covered cauliflower, every bit the right taste for a day of bright blue skies and Cyprus winter sunshine!

• Serves 4-6 •

Ingredients

1 large firm cauliflower
1oz (25g) butter
1-2 tablespoons light cooking oil, sunflower or grapeseed
½ glass/100ml dry red wine
salt and pepper
1 tablespoon freshly crushed coriander seeds

1. Wash the cauliflower and divide into small florets.

2. Melt the butter in a large frying pan, add the oil and fry the cauliflower gently until it begins to brown.

3. If there is still a lot of butter in the pan, remove the cauliflower and wipe the pan out. Replace the cauliflower and add the wine, seasoning and coriander.

4. Simmer covered until the cauliflower is cooked to your taste.

Serve cauliflower afelia as a side dish, or chilled as part of a mezze.

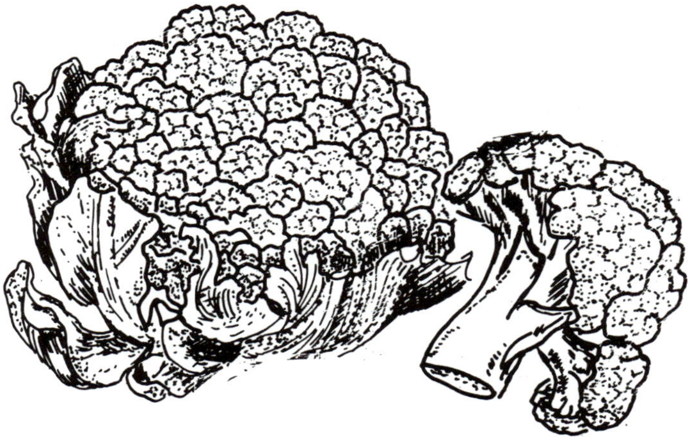

• Daktyla — Ladies Fingers •

These crisp, syrup soaked fingers of pastry which conceal an almond and cinnamon filling are now sold throughout the year in Cyprus although traditionally they should be made during Lent.

Xenia's mother, Koula, took me in hand when I suggested that daktyla were the sort of pastry that I thought I could make by myself. Wisely she didn't trust me further than the end of the kitchen, and soon I was completely under her culinary spell.

After the syrup Koula prepared the almond filling, then she made the dough. And all this in about 10 minutes. I was allowed to fill and roll the daktyla while the oil was heating.

How we laughed when my novice daktyla unrolled all over the frying pan and I then saw the wisdom in Koula's precise instructions.

• Makes about 2 dozen •

Ingredients

oil for deep frying

Pastry

2lb (1k) best quality flour
1 glass/200ml groundnut or sunflower oil
pinch of salt
about 2½ glasses/500ml lukewarm water

Filling

8oz (225g) almonds, blanched, skinned and chopped but not ground
4oz (100g) icing sugar
1 tablespoon ground cinnamon
1 teaspoon orange flower water
1 tablespoon water

Syrup

2 glasses/8oz granulated sugar
1½ glass/150ml water
juice of ½ lemon
2 tablespoons honey
2″ (5cm) stick of cinnamon

1. First prepare the syrup. Dissolve the sugar in the water and boil for 5 minutes. Add the remaining ingredients and leave to cool.

2. Mix all the ingredients for the filling.

3. To make the pastry, rub the oil into the flour until it is well mixed then pour in enough lukewarm water to make a soft dough. Knead well until quite smooth.

4. Take a tangerine size lump of dough and roll it on a floured board into a long strip about 4″ wide. It should be so thin that you can practically see through it. Cut the pastry into 4″ squares.

5. Put a teaspoon of filling in the middle of each piece of pastry and roll up like a cigar. Use a fork to seal both ends of the pastry encasing the nut filling in the middle.

6. Repeat this until you have used all the dough.

7. Heat the oil in a deep pan and fry a few pastries at a time until they are crisp and golden. Remove with a slotted spoon.

6. Immerse the daktyla immediately in the cool syrup for a minute then drain on kitchen paper. Serve well dusted with icing sugar, chopped almonds and a little ground cinnamon.

• Evie's Easter Biscuits •

Easter week and every household in Cyprus will be preparing biscuits for the Easter feast.

This recipe was given to me by Evie who cut my hair so well in Episkopi. It proved to be a total success with my family and neighbours and although the recipe makes a great many biscuits they were eaten before they had cooled on the rack.

You may prefer to halve the quantities.

• Makes between 2 and 3 dozen •

Ingredients

1 glass/200ml vegetable or sunflower oil
1 glass/4oz caster sugar
1 glass/4oz crushed almonds (leave the brown skins on and chop finely)
½ glass/2oz currants (optional)
2 eggs
2 teaspoons baking powder
½ teaspoon vanilla essence.
3-4 glasses/12-16oz plain flour

1. Mix all the ingredients until you have a firm paste.

2. Roll the mixture into small balls about the size of a walnut and place them on a baking sheet.

3. Flatten slightly with your hand before baking in a moderate oven Gas 4 350°F, 180°C for about 10 minutes.

4. Dust the biscuits with icing sugar as they cool and store in an airtight container.

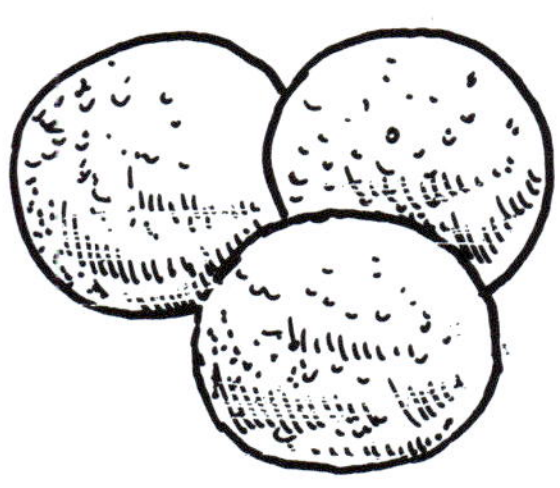

• Fakés Soupa — Lentil Soup •

This nourishing soup is traditionally eaten during Easter week. It contains vinegar because according to the scriptures, when Jesus asked for water on his way to Calvary He was given vinegar instead.

Lentils, or fakés as they are called in Cyprus have been used as a food since the Bronze Age in Egypt and India. They are one of the most useful pulses since they don't need to be soaked but can be cooked from dry.

• Serves 6 •

Ingredients

1 glass/5oz green lentils

5 glasses/1 litre water

4 spring onions, chopped

2 tablespoons leaf coriander or parsley, chopped

1 clove garlic

1 tablespoon olive oil

1 tablespoon plain flour blended with 2 tablespoons cold water

1-2 tablespoons wine vinegar

salt and pepper

1. Pick over the lentils and wash in several changes of water.

2. Put in a pan with water to cover, boil for 3 minutes and strain, discarding the water.

3. Place them in a large saucepan with a litre of cold water, spring onion, coriander, garlic and olive oil. Bring to the boil and simmer for 30-40 mins until the lentils are soft but not mushy.

4. Stir in the flour and water mixture, whisking hard all the time. Continue cooking the soup until it thickens.

5. Add vinegar to taste and seasonings. Don't be afraid of the vinegar, rather like adding half a glass of wine, it will just strengthen the flavour of the lentils.

• Flaounes — Easter Cheese Cakes •

Traditionally eaten to break the lenten fast Flaounes are, to me, the very best of Cypriot cooking. Cheesy buns with a soft rich filling and a crisp crust, just the thing to eat with a cup of coffee at breakfast or a glass of wine later in the day.

Flaounes are made by every family to celebrate Easter Day and bakeries now prepare miniature flaounes to sell throughout the year.

• Makes about 12 •

Ingredients

Yeast Dough

1½ lbs (750g) strong plain flour

1 sachet easy bake yeast

1 teaspoon salt

2 teaspoons sugar

2 tablespoons olive or vegetable oil

water to mix

Cheese Filling

8oz (250g) cheddar cheese or 12oz flaouna cheese if available

4oz (100g) halloumi

1 tablespoon flour

1 teaspoon baking powder

1 tablespoon crushed dried mint

4 eggs, lightly beaten

To finish

1 egg, beaten

sesame seeds

1. Sift flour into a large bowl. Stir in the yeast, salt and sugar. Add the oil and enough water to make a firm dough. Knead for at least 5 minutes until smooth and elastic. Put the dough in a plastic bag and leave in a warm place for an hour to rise.

2. For the filling, coarsely grate the cheeses, add the flour and baking powder then gradually stir in the beaten egg and seasonings until you have a stiffish paste (keep some of the beaten egg back if the mixture becomes too runny.

3. Divide the dough into egg sized pieces and roll these into 4″ (10cm) discs.

4. Place a generous tablespoon of filling in the centre of each pastry disc, spreading it slightly. Pull dough up at 3 points to make a triangle, or 4 points to make a square. You should still be able to see the filling in the middle.

5. Press corners together to seal and leave to rise. Just before baking brush with beaten egg and sprinkle some sesame seeds over the finished flaounes.

6. Bake in a hot oven Gas 8, 450°C, 230°C for 12-15 minutes until cheese filling is puffed and flaounes are golden.

Serve warm or cold.

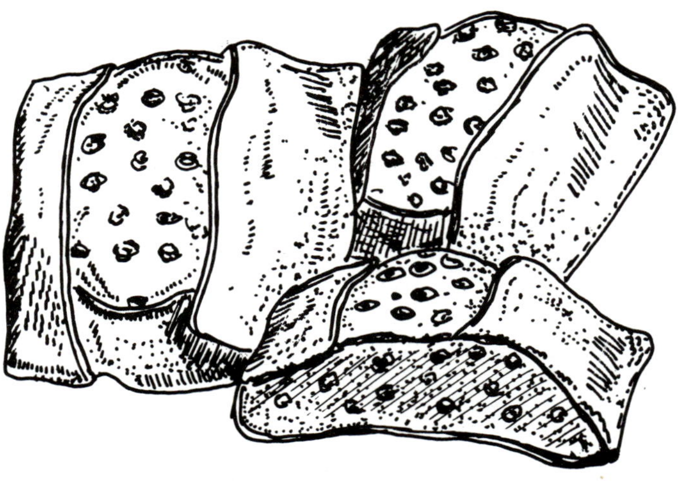

• Hirino Me Kolokassi — Pork with Kolokassi •

"Oh it's a Cyprus sweet potato" said the stall holders when I first met up with kolokassi in the market. It looked possible but I doubted it, especially when I was given the cooking instructions.

> "Take care, don't allow the vegetable to get wet as it becomes slimy, and chip it rather than chop it into the frying pan!"

Tasting rich and pleasant when cooked in a pork casserole with tomato and celery I was more than intrigued to discover the origins of this mysterious vegetable!

Many reference books and a great many questions later revealed that Kolokassi is in fact the taro (Colocasia esculenta) native to the Pacific Islands, and I am told that there is a village called Kolokassi near Kyrenia on the north coast. But how did it arrive in Cyprus? . . . answers on a post card please!

Perhaps Kolokassi is stocked at your local Cypriot grocers or on the exotic vegetable counter in your supermarket, if not then substitute parsnip.

• Serves 6 •

Ingredients

2lb (1kg) boneless stewing pork
4 tablespoons oil
1 large onion, diced
3 sticks celery, chopped
3-4 tablespoons tomato puree dissolved in a glass of hot water
salt and pepper
2lbs (1 kg) kolokassi (taro)
juice of ½ lemon

1. Cut pork into a ¾″ (2cm) cubes.

2. Heat half the oil in a heavy pan and brown pork cubes, transferring to a plate when browned.

3. Reduce heat, add remaining oil, onion and celery and fry gently until soft. Add tomato puree and bring to the boil, stirring well.

4. Return meat to pan and cook gently for 1½ hours.

5. Scrub kolokassi, dry well with paper towels and peel. Chip off pieces and put on top of the meat.

6. Sprinkle over the lemon juice, and add a little water if necessary. Don't stir the kolokassi but cover the pot and continue to cook for a further 30-40 minutes until pork and vegetables are tender.

7. Skim off excess fat, taste for seasoning and serve kolokassi with rice or potatoes.

• Kolokotes •

I first came across Kolokotes one morning when hunger caught up with me after jostling through the crowded market in Limassol.

Golden brown pastries, half-moon shaped, and, the stall holder informed me, full of red marrow and wheat. The description had me reaching for my purse!

Inside my pastry case I discovered cubes of pumpkin, pourgouri or cracked wheat and a few raisins. Could this be an adaptation from the American Pumpkin Pie, because I can link it to no other source in the Middle East?

Kolokotes are made in most homes during the fasting period before Christmas and Easter, when the sweet marrows or pumpkins are available. They are a fine compensation for the non meat-eating population.

• Makes about 12 •

Ingredients

Filling

1lb (450g) sweet red marrow or pumpkin, peeled and diced)

1 tablespoon sultanas or raisins

2 tablespoons pourgouri (cracked wheat)

½ onion, finely chopped

2 tablespoons vegetable oil

½ teaspoon ground cinnamon

salt, pepper and sugar to taste

Pastry

4 glasses/1lb plain flour

pinch of salt

¾ glass/6 tablespoons vegetable or sunflower oil (or 6oz melted butter)

½ glass/4 tablespoons cold water

1 tablespoon lemon juice

beaten egg and milk for glazing

1. Mix all the ingredients for the filling and leave overnight.

2. Make up the pastry; Sift flour with salt. Pour oil or melted fat into flour and combine well with fingertips or, better still, in a food processor. Pour in lemon juice and cold water and mix to a firm dough. Chill for 30 minutes.

3. Break off little lumps of pastry about the size of a walnut and roll these into 6″ discs.

4. Place a tablespoon of the filling just to one side of the centre, fold half the pastry over to form a lid and press the edges together to make a half moon shape. Curl the edges of the pastry back towards the pastry making a raised lip.

5. Brush kolokotes with a mixture of beaten egg and milk, and bake them on a lightly greased baking tray in a moderate oven 350°F, 180°C for about 20 minutes.

Serve hot or cold. I like them best with a spoonful of plain yogurt.

• Louvia Me Lahana — Black-Eyed Bean with Greens •

This is a typical Cypriot dish that is served in the Spring. At this time of the year, after the winter rains, the leafy green vegetables are at their best. Chard leaves with their white fleshy stems give a crunchy texture to the black eyed beans and make this a substantial dish to serve on its own, together as part of a hot meal, or cool as a salad or first course.

Black eyed beans are called *louvi mavromati* in Cyprus. They are a cousin of the cowpea family, and native to central Africa. Black eyed beans have a pleasant, slightly sweet flavour and cook more quickly than other dried beans. A tablespoon of lemon juice added to the cooking liquid stops the beans discolouring, but I find this sometimes makes them tough and prefer to add lemon juice at the end with the oil. My louvia have a rather muddy healthy look!

Since they need no soaking the whole dish can be prepared within half an hour.

• Serves 4-6 •

Ingredients

2 glasses/8oz black-eyed beans, picked clean and washed

1lb or 1 bunch chard leaves (fresh spinach makes a good alternative)

olive oil and lemon juice to serve with the beans.

1. In a largish saucepan, cover the beans with water and bring to the boil. Drain and throw the water away.

2. Cover with fresh water and simmer for about 25 minutes, or until almost tender, adding more water if necessary to keep the beans covered.

3. Shred the spinach or chard leaves and toss into the beans. Cook for a further five minutes.

4. Season the beans well with salt and pepper.

5. Serve Louvia me Lahana hot, warm or cold with a good spoonful of olive oil and lots and lots of fresh lemon juice squeezed over them.

I like this dish served with some sharp plain yogurt.

It is an ideal first course for a hot day or as part of a barbecue or main meal.

• Octapodi Krassato — Octopus in Red Wine •

"He plunged once more into the boot of the car and emerged with a bottle of ouzo and a length of yellow hosepipe which I recognized as dried octopus. We sat beside the road in the thin spring sunshine and shared a stirrup-cup and a meze while he told me, not only all he knew about Amathus, but all about himself and his family with an attention to details which would have been less wearying perhaps were I planning a novel".

Lawrence Durrel in BITTER LEMONS.

A live octopus wriggling around on the quay side is one thing, and a beaten, cleaned and prepared octopus is another. I suggest you observe the former and cook the latter!

The success or failure of this dish lies with the tenderness of the octopus. Quiz your fishmonger carefully before buying. I have made this dish with frozen octopus, and it worked well.

In Cyprus squid and cuttlefish are also cooked 'Krassato'.

• Serves 4-6 •

Ingredients

1 octopus of about 2lbs/1kg weight
2 large onions, chopped
½ glass/100ml olive oil
2 tablespoons red-wine vinegar
2 glasses/400ml dry red wine
4 medium tomatoes, grated
1 tablespoon tomato puree
1 bay leaf
1 stick of cinnamon
2 cloves
salt and black pepper

1. Put the octopus in a pan over medium heat. It will turn red as it cooks in its own juices. Leave it for about 5 minutes then take it out and chop into bite sized pieces.

2. In a heavy based casserole, heat the oil, brown the pieces of octopus slightly then add the onions, let them colour to golden then add all the remaining ingredients.

3. Cover and simmer gently for 2-3 hours until the octopus is tender.

Serve the dish as it is, or dish up the octopus and sieve the sauce before pouring it on top. I like octopus krassato hot or cold.

• Elioti — Cypriot Olive Bread •

This is a traditional loaf baked during Lent when according to the Greek Orthodox Calendar, Cypriots adhere to a strict fast. It is full of flavour and very moist due to the oil and chopped olives it envelopes.

Although many Cypriot housewives now cook on gas, eliot tastes particularly good when it comes freshly baked from one of the traditional 'beehive' ovens. These spacious outdoor bread ovens are still used, especially in the villages where neighbours combine their baking days and share the heat. A wood fire is lit inside the large oven and once the walls and floor are hot enough the glowing embers can be scraped out. Prepared loaves are carefully arranged on the floor with the use of a long handled spatula. The ovens are then sealed with a door or large stone and timings may be unpredictable, but with experience the baked loaves turn out remarkably well.

• Makes a 2lb loaf •

Ingredients

1lb (450g) strong white bread flour

8oz (225g) stoneground wholemeal flour

1 sachet easy blend yeast

2 teaspoons salt

2 tablespoons olive oil

about 2 glasses or ¾ pint water, at blood heat

Filling

1 medium onion, chopped and lightly fried in olive oil

1 tablespoon olive oil

7oz/200g stoned, chopped black olives

1. Using an electric mixer or food processor, tip all the flour into the bowl and stir in the yeast and salt.

2. Switch on and pour in the oil and enough water to make a soft but not sticky dough. Adjust water and a little more flour if necessary.

3. Knead the dough until it becomes smooth and elastic.

4. Turn the dough into an oiled bowl, cover with a polythene bag and leave in a warm place for about an hour or until it has doubled in size.

5. Turn the dough onto a floured board or table top and knead it again for a minute before adding the cooked onion, extra oil and chopped olives.

6. Shape the dough into a round loaf, place on an oiled baking tray and cover again with a large polythene bag. Leave to rise for ½ an hour.

7. Preheat the oven to Gas 4, 350°F, 180°C and bake the Elioti for about 45 minutes or until the base sounds hollow when tapped.

8. Brush the top lightly with oil and return to the oven for a minute to make the top shiny.

• Pitta Bread •

The hard grain wheat grown in Cyprus has a high gluten content and is ideal for making bread. Compared to the basic village bread which is subsidized by the government and sells for as little as 15 cents, about 18p, pitta bread is relatively expensive. Each piece costs 10 cents.

Another flat bread that has become popular in Cyprus is the disc of Lebanese bread which has a slightly chewy texture. It is produced mainly in Limassol where the majority of Lebanese have settled since the troubles began in Lebanon.

Pitta bread needs to be cooked in the hottest part of the oven for it to puff and make a hollow pocket in the middle. It can be cooked successfully in an electric frying pan.

Fresh yeast is a fairly rare commodity in Cyprus so I use an easy blend yeast which goes straight into the flour.

• Makes 12 •

Ingredients

1½ lbs (750g) strong white bread flour
1 sachet of easy blend yeast
2 teaspoons salt
2 tablespoons olive oil
about 2 glasses/400ml water, at blood heat

1. Sift the flour into the mixing bowl. Add the yeast and salt and stir well to distribute.

2. Add the oil and then most of the water. Mix and knead for 5 minutes until you have a good bread dough, still quite damp but not so that it sticks to your hands. Adjust water and extra flour.

3. Put dough into a lightly oiled bowl and cover with a large plastic bag. Leave in a warm place until doubled in size — at least an hour.

4. Preheat the oven to its hottest. Place two oven trays near the top. Oil two baking trays.

5. Divide the dough into 12. Knead each piece into a smooth ball then roll out into an oval about 7″ (18cm) long. Leave on a floured worktop for ½ hour to prove.

6. Preheat the oiled baking trays then slip 3 pittas quickly onto each. Sprinkle them with water and put them back into the oven immediately. Bake for between 3 and 5 minutes. They should be brown but not hard. Wrap the cooked pitta in a clean cloth and bake the remaining dough.

• Patates Spastes—Potatoes with Wine •

Cyprus potatoes are well known in Britain since they arrive with the best of the 'earlies'. With a good flavour and a firm texture they make the most perfect chips.

You can always tell a Cyprus potato because it wears a reddish coat from the rich Cypriot soil. Apart from chips, the Cypriots incorporate potatoes in many roast and casserole dishes but this recipe for potatoes with wine is a great favourite.

• Serves 4-6 •

Ingredients

1 ½ lb (700g) small potatoes, scrubbed
1 glass/200ml sunflower or vegetable oil
3 tablespoons olive oil
2 tablespoons coriander seeds, crushed coarsely
salt and freshly ground pepper
1 glass/100ml dry red wine

1. Using a wooden mallet or pestle, hit the potatoes, a few at a time, on a chopping board. They should not disintegrate but crack slightly. Dry on kitchen paper.

2. Heat the oil and deep fry the potatoes in batches until golden all over — about 3-4 mins. Drain.

3. Gently heat the olive oil in a heavy saucepan, add the coriander and seasoning, then the potatoes.

4. Turn them over to coat them with the coriander and pour in the wine. Cover the saucepan and cook gently for about 20 minutes, until the potatoes are done to your taste, tossing occasionally in order to prevent them from sticking.

• Ravioles •

Pasta in Cyprus! Surely this is an Italian influence dating back to the Venetian or Genoese occupation of the island during the 13th and 14th century? Probably, but similar pasta dishes are found in Greece, Turkey, Armenia, Iran and Afghanistan. So let's think further back to ancient China, or was it the Mongol influence which drifted eastwards from Persia or the Caucasus.

Ravioles in Cyprus are very much a lenten dish, made by everyone in great numbers during carnival week. Fear not though, for as with all successful dishes, the Cypriots now serve ravioles all the year round, often as part of a meze.

• Serves 4-6 •

Ingredients

Dough

4 glasses/1lb plain flour

1 teaspoon salt

2 eggs, lightly beaten

about ¾–1 glass/150-200ml cold water

Cheese Filling

7oz (200g) halloumi cheese, grated (use gruyere type cheese as alternative)

4oz/100g cottage cheese, fresh anari or ricotta

2 eggs

1-2 teaspoons dried mint

To finish

boiling salted water

3oz/75g melted butter

grated halloumi or cheddar

1. Sift flour and salt into a large bowl or food processor. Add eggs and enough water to make a soft dough. Turn onto floured board, knead well for 10 minutes until smooth and elastic. Rest dough for an hour.

2. Mix ingredients for filling, adding mint to taste.

3. Divide pastry into 4. Roll out into long strips about 3″ (8cm) wide.

4. Place a teaspoon of filling every 1½× (4cm) down the strip, slightly to one side of centre.

5. Brush some water down the edges of the pastry. Fold over to cover the filling and cut crescent shapes around the filling. (Cypriot cooks use the rim of a glass to cut this shape). Seal the pastry edges with the prongs of a fork.

6. Cook about 15 ravioles at a time in a large pot of boiling stock for 15-20 minutes or until tender. Remove with a slotted spoon to keep warm.

7. When all the ravioles are cooked, pour over the melted butter and sprinkle with grated cheese.

• Pilaf — Rice with Mushrooms •

This recipe was given to me by a Cypriot friend whose English wasn't particularly strong, but she kindly wrote out the instructions for me as best she could. As I read her words I can see her gentle, rather shy, smiling face. These are her words, which, of course, make complete sense to any cook.

"You put the butter or oil to hot and drop the onion that grind before and you leave them about 5 minutes".

• Serves 4-6 •

Ingredients

2 glasses/10oz long grain rice
4 tablespoons oil or 3oz butter
4 glasses/800mls light stock
2 onions, grated
8oz/225g tomatoes
8oz/225g mushrooms
salt and pepper
2oz hard cheese, parmesan or dry anari, grated
2 tablespoons chopped parsley - to garnish

1. Heat half of the oil or butter and fry the onion gently for about 5 minutes.

2. Stir in the rice and cook for another 3 minutes. Heat the stock and pour in, turn the heat down, cover and simmer the rice for about 18 minutes.

3. Meanwhile cover the tomatoes with boiling water, count to 10, drain the tomatoes under cold running water and peel. Quarter and deseed.

4. Keep a few mushrooms for decoration, slice the rest.

5. Heat the rest of the oil or butter and fry the tomatoes and mushrooms, season well and stir in the cheese.

6. When the rice is cooked stir in the tomato mixture and press the rice into a bowl or mould. Turn out on to a serving dish and decorate with the remaining mushrooms and parsley and serve with natural yogurt.

• Skordalia — Garlic Sauce •

This is the most basic dip imaginable. Garlic may dominate the initial taste but wait until the sweet ground almond aftertaste catches up with you!

Skordalia dates back to medieval times and beyond, and still appears in kitchens all over the Middle East. Pine nuts are used in the Lebanon, Syria and Egypt while ground walnuts flavour the Turkish Tarator sauce. Skordalia can be served as a sauce with fried fish or vegetables, or simply as it is.

• Serves 4-6 •

Ingredients

2oz (50g) whole almonds, blanched with brown skins removed

3 slices white bread, crusts removed

2 cloves garlic, finely chopped and crushed with a little salt

1 tablespoon white wine vinegar or lemon juice

4-5 tablespoons olive oil

garnish with black olives

1. Soak the bread in cold water for 5 minutes.
2. In a liquidiser or food processor, chop the almonds finely.
3. Squeeze the bread to drain excess water and add to ground almonds with the garlic, vinegar and almonds.
4. Add enough oil to make a fairly runny consistency, adding a little water if necessary.
5. Serve the skordalia in a bowl, garnished with olives and lots of fresh vegetables to dip in.

• Stir Fry Greens •

The first day of lent in the Greek Orthodox calendar is known as Kathari Deftera. This public holiday follows the two weeks of fun and feasting during the carnival, when body and soul both need a purge. So after a good spring clean through the house most Cypriots drive into the countryside to 'get away from it all'.

Olives, wine, bread and vegetables are the diet for the day. Often the wild greens are gathered by the whole family who look for leaves from the mallow plant, **moloshes,** or wild asparagus **agrelia.**

(I like these greens best simply stir-fried in olive oil and bound together with a lightly beaten egg. Served with some fresh bread and a glass or two of local wine, delicious!)

• Serves 4 •

Ingredients

2lb (1k) fresh young spring greens, spinach or very young asparagus

2 tablespoons olive oil

4 eggs

salt and freshly ground black pepper

1. Wash and shred the greens by pulling them apart with your hands. Drain well.

2. In a large frying pan heat the oil and stir fry the greens until they begin to wilt.

3. Beat the eggs lightly together with a tablespoon of water and pour into the greens. Stir continuously as the egg begins to set.

4. Season well with salt and pepper and turn the omelette out onto warm plates.

5. In Cyprus this dish would always be served with a fresh lemon to squeeze and a chunk of fresh bread. A full bodied wine seems right too!

• Taramosalata – Smoked Cod's Roe Paté •

Pale pink and rather insipid, slightly salty, or maybe sharp with lemon juice; shop bought Taramosalata is not a patch on the real thing! Alas, taverna owners all too often rely on undiscerning visitors and buy in their pink squidge.

Tarama is the dried, salt pressed and lightly smoked roe of the grey mullet. Sadly, even here in the Levant, natural habitat of the grey mullet, the roe has always been expensive. You may be lucky to find some vivid orange smoked mullet roe, if not, then settle for the smoked roe from cod which is a deep reddish pink.

Delicatessens, good fishmongers and the large chain stores stock tarama.

• Serves 6-8 •

Ingredients

4oz (100g) tarama
4 slices day-old bread, crusts removed
1 clove garlic, crushed with a pinch of salt
juice of 1 lemon
6-8 tablespoons olive oil
4 tablespoons cold water
pinch of paprika, to improve colour if necessary

1. Soak the bread in cold water for 5 minutes, squeeze dry.

2. Skin the roe if necessary. Using a food processor or whisk, combine the roe, bread, garlic and lemon juice.

3. Add olive oil and water by the spoonful, alternatively until the mixture is thick and creamy. Add paprika.

Serve taramosalata with slivers of warm pitta bread. The toaster crisps them well!

Summer

In the sweltering heat of a Cyprus summer, while tourists arrive every hour of the day to soak up the seaside and sunshine, just watch the Cypriots head inland and take a trip to the hills. The temperature and humidity are a great deal lower here and a day away from the coast acts as a health cure to the heat weary.

This is the ideal time to visit a Cyprus village and catch up on some of the rural activities that go on today just as they did a century ago. Come with me to visit a village in the Pitsilia region, high up on the slopes of Troodos above Limassol.

When I first visited Agros it was the beginning of June and I found the village bathed in peacefulness and the scent of roses. The streets were rather empty, not much hustle and bustle, no idle gossip in the coffee shops, for most of the inhabitants were at work and the children at school. Agros is a busy and growing village, which is rather unusual in Cyprus. For de-population is the theme of most rural communities, as the young villagers must travel to school and then travel again to find employment. But in Agros with 1,200 inhabitants, there is both a primary and senior school and work for all who choose.

Since the Xyliatos dam was built in 1977 the area has gone from rags to riches. The area is now opulent in agriculture, growing mainly deciduous fruit trees such as apples, pears, plums, peaches, cherries, and, more recently, kiwi fruit, and nuts of all kinds. Yes, even pistachio nuts as well as almonds, walnuts and hazelnuts, and of course olives with some new varieties as an experiment.

Grape vines, naturally, play a vital part in the village community, with almost every family being involved with viticulture. After the autumn grape picking, most of the wine grapes are taken to the large wineries in Limassol to be processed. Extremely potent and delicious, though, is the wine made locally in the village by traditional methods. Agros village wine flows liberally during the August village fete and the flavour may vary enormously from vineyard to vineyard now that so many new grape varieties have been introduced. Well worth a visit for a wine-tasting I should say!

Over the past few years the enterprising inhabitants of Agros have formed a co-operative. Their first project was to build the **Rhoden** or Rose Hotel. Land has been made available to property investors, a lively cultural centre opened, redevelopment of the present health centre took place and the approach roads to Agros were immensely improved to help attract visitors. One or two industrious villagers have made a commercial business out of the traditional art of **pork curing.** Buying pigs from the valley village of Orunda, they cure the pork in Agros village wine and then press and smoke it over a three month period. **Lounza,** the smoked fillet, **hiromeri,** the cured and smoked gammon, and **loukanika** sausages, made from fresh pork flavoured with coriander seeds, all are produced in Agros and then delivered to a number of outlets in Limassol, Larnaca and Nicosia.

Another growing village concern is the traditional art of making Cyprus sweets or **glyko,** which are fresh fruits preserved in syrup. This is not as simple as it seems, and preparations go on for a couple of days for each fruit. All the most unusual glyko is now being prepared; green walnuts, cherries, figs, melon peel, citrus fruit peel. Even if you don't have a particularly sweet tooth, don't leave Cyprus without giving these delicacies a try, perhaps a less common one to look out for though, is glyko made from rose petals.

Rose-water and Agros are fast becoming synonymous to many people. For the production of this fragrant distillation for culinary purposes has done much to save the very soul of a dying village. The reason behind the success of rosewater is that there will always be a market for it — Arab countries, throughout the Middle East,

Turkey, Greece, even Australia, Europe and especially Britain need rosewater.

Eat any sticky pastry in the Levant, be it a Daktyla, Bourekia, Kateyfi, or Baklava — it will, no doubt, be soaked in aromatic and sweet scented rose water. Taste any milk pudding or fruit compote and again, rosewater will be an essential ingredient . . . in fact, here in Cyprus, every household must buy a bottle of rose water at least once a year. No wonder that the income from the rose water co-operative in Agros is £20,000 in just the six week period during which the roses flower.

Let me give you a 'day in the life' of the rose on the day it meets its distillation.

Picking starts at dawn during the six week period of May to June when the Damascus roses bloom.

The multi-petalled pale pink roses are heavily scented and as they amass in their baskets ready to be weighed, the air is truly heady.

Once the roses contributed by each farmer have been registered they are tipped into the bottom of a large metal vat with twice their weight of water. The boilers are lit and a moderate temperature is maintained throughout the distillation. As soon as the water boils, the steam from the heating roses rises to the top of the container. Here it condenses into droplets because the lid of the vat is chilled by a constant supply of cold water from above. So the droplets of rosewater are drained off and collected before being bottled and labelled.

So simple, yet so successful.

Have **you** got a fresh bottle in the larder?

ORDER A MEZÉ

"I raised the demijohn of wine and gave him the traditional Cypriot greeting, Kopiaste, sit down and join us."

Lawrence Durrell in Bitter Lemons.

Share a Mezé in Cyprus and you have tasted the true flavours of the island.

There's no better way to discover Cypriot cooking than by nibbling at a variety of bits and pieces during the course of an evening.

So settle yourself down in a cool taverna on the coast, and as the sun sets on the sea, pour the wine, pick at the olives and relax.

MEZÉ is short for Mezedhes or little delicacies and wherever you travel around the Mediterranean they appear in some form or other.

Tapas are traditional in Spain, in France the first course of a meal is usually a small tasty 'nibble', and in Greece no drink could be served without a small bowl of olives.

Throughout the Middle East purees of pulses make an ideal and moorish dip for crisp warm unleaven bread or pitta as does Dukka, those wonderful mixtures of crushed roasted seeds, nuts and herbs.

In Cyprus a mezé is a complete meal. In fact, it is so tempting to attack each dish as it arrives, one often feels that they have eaten for a week by the end! Take a leaf out of a Cypriot's book and take your mezé *"siga siga"* or slowly slowly.

So, the decision has been made and your mezé is ordered. What can you expect to eat?

First comes the olives, black and green, **elies tsakistes** with a dressing of lemon, garlic, herbs and oil.

Dips of **tahini, skordalia, taramosalata,** and **zanziki** arrive with a basket of fresh village bread and a bowl of **salata khoriatiki** village salad.

Octapodhi krassato octopus in red wine, **karaoli yachni** snails in tomato sauce, **zalatina** brawn and pickles of capers **kappari** and cauliflower **moungra** are some of the more unusual mezé dishes that may arrive now.

Bunches of greens, some raw, some dressed with lemon juice and salt such as carrots and kohlrabi, and some tossed in oil and bound with egg may fit into your mezé at this point.

Fish of some kind may appear at this stage. **Marida** tiny sardine type fish or **barbouni** red mullet which are usually served very small, and **kalamari** or rings of squid are battered and deep fried, accompanied with chunks of fresh lemons.

Grilled **halloumi** cheese and **lounza** the smoked pork come next followed by **keftedes** meat balls **sheftalia** pork rissoles and **loukanika** smoked Cyprus sausages.

Now for the composite dishes or casseroles such as **afelia, moussaka** and **stifado.**

Towards the end of the meal come the kebabs or **souvlakia** as well as lamb chops and pieces of chicken, arriving straight from the grill. But perhaps you are beginning to feel full now?

No surprise — well done — after all you've survived your first meze! Sit back contented in the knowledge that little else is to follow. Just some fresh fruit, carefully prepared and segmented and well, and perhaps just a few **bourekia** filled with fresh cured cheese and honey.

No more . . . I hear you beg!

VISIT A MARKET

Before the sun rises too high in the sky and Cyprus begins to shimmer with heat, let's take a trip to the market.

Which way? just follow any of the bustling black clad old ladies armed with shopping bags or the more leisurely old men who shop early to gather fresh provisions for the day.

Most of the items in the Cypriot market will be familiar but some may be quite new to you, and this is when the fun starts. Carry a dictionary if you can, or even better borrow a translator for the day! If you have neither, don't worry, there will be many friendly smiles and nods of encouragement as well as a taste of anything you like.

Let's start with the fruit and vegetables. Have you ever seen such enormous mounds of glistening fresh produce? And fresh it is, for most will have only been picked a few hours earlier. You won't find any imported goods though, only those fruit and vegetables which are grown here on the island. Just look at those tomatoes, sun ripened and so full of flavour! Crates full of peppers, courgettes, aubergines and avocado pears.

Salad stuffs and fresh herbs in untidy bundles such as purslane, rocket and leaf coriander. Then there are some more exotic vegetables; okra, swiss chard, fresh black eye beans and artichokes. But what is **colocassi?** This is a root vegetable rather like a sweet potato and a speciality of Cyprus. It has a rich flavour and is especially good with pork.

More than likely you will be offered some fresh fruit to nibble as you wander through the stalls; a generous offer given without any pressure or compulsion to buy. Even after the glut of citrus fruit in the spring there are still oranges, grapefruits and lemons in the market during the summer. Strawberries, which first appear in January and February are still available during the summer months, but only those grown in the mountain villages. Enormous black cherries come in during June as do plums, apricots, peaches and nectarines. August is the month for water melons, at 60p a kilo they are a juicy refreshing bargain. Sweet pipless grapes flood the market from July to November and they are a refreshing snack to take to the beach.

But my favourite fruit of all are the green and purple figs that ripen towards the end of the summer and burst open to reveal a magic array of colourful seeds.

Fish is a good buy at the market. Often an expensive dish in a restaurant but if you can cook it yourself then buy as many varieties as you can find. Red mullet or **barbouni** as it is called in Greek, sea-bream or **fangri,** whitebait which is **marides,** sea bass known as **sphyrida** or **xyphia** the delicious swordfish. Enjoy them all but perhaps leave the preparation of the trickier fish like octopus and squid for the tavernas. Let them do all the hard work, for they serve these fish in a variety of delicious ways.

Moving on to the meat stalls, don't be offended by the sight of red carcasses, after all, what self respecting cook should accept their meat neatly wrapped in polythene? The meat in Cyprus is eaten very fresh, hardly hung at all, and you may well notice the difference in flavour. Lamb and beef are lean and tasty but can be expensive compared to pork which is extremely good value and of excellent quality. Kebabs or **souvlakia** are usually made from pork in Cyprus but **souvla,** the chunks of meat grilled on a spit are prepared from lamb or goat. Goat is the same price as lamb and I find it a lean tasty meat, ideal for grilling, or cooking in the kleftico as most Cypriots do.

Offal is well priced and much loved by the Cypriots, who are thrifty people and allow nothing to go to waste.

Lastly, perhaps the most interesting section of all. The delicatessen department which sells a variety of goods supplied from small producers in the mountain villages. What are all those sausages hanging up, I hear you ask? Perhaps **loukanika,** the Cypriot sausage. There are many different types and flavours of loukanika, as not only each village but also each family has its own recipe. The meat content is very high and usually crushed coriander and other spices are added to them. Before being smoked the sausages are soaked in red wine. Loukanika taste good when fried or grilled. Another smoked pork product is **hiromeri,** leg of pork which is marinated and spiced like the loukanika, as is **lounza,** the delicious fillet of pork. A favourite with the Cypriots is **pastourma,** a reminder of the Armenian influence. They contain a lot of chilli pepper, paprika and ground fenugreek and add a spicy bit to a barbecue.

All these speciality pork dishes may appear in your taverna mezé, but to ensure that you taste them buy a little of each; they make an ideal snack or component for a picnic. As for the cheeses, ask to taste the more unusual hard cheeses like **kefalotyri** or **kashkaval.** These and other cheese like **feta, halloumi** and **anari** are best bought here in the market. They will probably be home made and have real character to them; ask about their origin and you will be locked into a fascinating discussion for at least half an hour!

Peep into the sacks of pulses stacked in front of you to discover a wide range of beans and dried peas. Prepared more often in Cypriot homes than restaurants, they make up a substantial part of the Cypriot diet. **Fasoulia** is a traditional dish made from haricot beans served with olive oil and fresh lemon juice, or **louvia** which are the black eyed beans cooked with fresh green vegetables.

Pickles are popular and jars with unusual contents may catch your eye. One of the greatest delicacies in Cyprus are **ambelopoulia** or pickled birds. Although they may not appeal to visitors the pickling of these little birds known as becaficos is said to have been introduced by the Knights Hospitallier as far back as the thirteenth century.

Nuts, honey and so many more good things, but by now your hunger must be reaching a crescendo. So gather your bags and wander away from the hustle and bustle of the inner market halls. But don't go too fast; why not stop and tend to those desperate pangs of hunger. Here is a street vendor with his wooden 'Heath Robinson contraption' from which he sells something that smells just too good to pass by. Fresh bread, **olive buns, tahini pies, flaounas** or **halloumi pastries** and even sausage rolls . . . go on, let yourself be tempted!

Look out for delicious almond filled **daktyla** or ladies fingers, honey soaked **loukmades** which look a little like doughnuts or **pishides** which literally drip with orange flower water syrup.

My favourite market 'bite' is a **koupa.** This is quite special and should be tasted by every visitor to Cyprus. Resembling a stubby cigar it is brown in colour and has a crisp outer coating of pourgouri or cracked wheat which has been made into a paste with water. Inside each deep fried cigar is some spiced minced meat mixed with onions and parsley. As you bite into your koupa, enjoy the combination of flavours and textures of spicy filling and crisp casing. Adding a good squeeze of lemon juice once you have bitten off the top is a clever local habit.

So now that you have arms laden with bags and hands full of pastries, a wise move would be to forsake the market in search of a shaded cafe. As you slump into your chair, and a tray of reviving cool drinks arrive at the table; relax. Peel back the wrapping around those pastries, and little by little nibble your way through a whole host of tastes and flavours. With the heat and excitement of the morning behind you, sit back and enjoy the fruits of your trip to the market.

A WEDDING IN CYPRUS

Branches of orange, lovely with flowers
Seven are the bridesmaids who sew the bed
Into the brides hall flew two nightingales
They came to bring her English needles

Wedding verse (Cypriot Greek bridal song)

A Cypriot wedding is something very special and if you should be lucky enough to be invited to one — then you will know!

For the visitor to Cyprus though, who spends just a couple of weeks enjoying the sunshine and island, there is an easy way to see the various wedding customs performed by one of the many traditional dance groups. Just visit one of the popular tavernas which offer live entertainment and the dancers will give you a clear picture of the lively preparations made for a Cypriot wedding.

Weddings in Cyprus today vary from the traditional village marriage that hasn't changed for centuries to the more modern European style. A traditional wedding could still be pre-arranged between families and the dowry for the bride may have been set aside since her birth. Whereas the future groom gives his education and trade to the pact, the bride should provide the house and furniture, or at least the land on which to build a home. A family with say three daughters must plan carefully to provide each with a dowry for their future happiness and this can stretch a rural community to hardship.

A more modern approach suits many Cypriot couples these days especially if both bride and groom work and can contribute to their future house and home. But most families like to own a little land so that they can provide at least a base for their children.

The rituals and traditions of a Cypriot wedding are such fun that most couples like to include as many as possible, and the first of these is the engagement party. After a blessing in the church the families gather to celebrate and make plans.

Invitations go out to as many people as possible, recently in the hills above Paphos over 3,000 guests attended a summer wedding.

In the past invitations would have been given by the bride's mother who prepared a specially decorated pastry ring to offer to each guest. Handkerchiefs were used as invitations too.

Weddings are family affairs and everyone loves to be involved. The feast is prepared by as many friends and neighbours as possible and may take over a week to cook.

Ressi is the traditional meal to serve at weddings. It is a kind of Cyprus pilaff and has been served at special occasions for hundreds of years. There is a saying in the villages that goes "a wedding without ressi is like winter without rain".

The ingredients for ressi are lamb, wheat, chicken and the fat from the tail of a special breed of lamb. Ressi should be cooked for at least 5-6 hours until the meat literally melts into the wheat and the final dish looks rather like porridge. It has a very special taste and I think it is delicious. Other dishes prepared for the wedding feast are **pasticcio, psito** (roast meat with potatoes), **keftedes (meat balls) and koupepia** (stuffed vine leaves) as well as salads.

Loukoumi, little sugar covered shortbreads with almonds in the centre are baked then wrapped in cellophane with ribbons ready for the guests. Needless to say, during all the preparations there is lots of fun with dancing and singing amongst the many friends involved. In the most traditional villages many of the jobs, such as grinding the wheat, must be performed by the young and the wheat should be washed in the village fountain up to seven times.

The bridal mattress gets special attention and ribbons are sewn to it. A small boy is rolled across it and then the bride and groom's mothers lay the sheets on the bed. Although this is more of a colourful

ritual these days the hope of the first born being a boy is indicative of the male dominant society in Cyprus.

The wedding ceremony is gay and noisy, with lots of involvement with all the guests. The bride wears white these days but red used to be the wedding colour since it is the colour for joy.

The reception is a seated affair which may last for hours and hours but no one leaves for fear of missing the main feature of the wedding, the **"ploumisma"** or presenting of money.

After the wedding feast the bride and groom take to the dance floor and as they dance guests pin money on to their clothes. They are literally covered from head to foot and the total amount gives the couple a healthy start to married life.

• Baklava •

Baklava is very Middle Eastern with its wafer thin sheets of crisp filo pastry, layered with nuts and honey.

In Turkey you may find that the nuts are walnuts, while pistachio are used more often in the Lebanon and Arab countries. In Cyprus, almonds are used in baklava since they are indigenous to the island. Pistachio nuts are being grown as an experiment, so maybe your Cypriot baklava may soon have green nuts in it too.

It seems likely that baklava is of true Greek origin for although the Turks occupied Greece for 400 years and could have well introduced it, the Greek writer Athenaeos wrote about baklava in the second century AD. Does this make it almost the oldest known Greek dessert?

• Makes large trayful •

Ingredients

1 lb (½ kilo) 'filo' pastry
½ glass/100g melted butter

For the filling
3oz (75g) butter
3oz (75g) sugar
1 glass/100ml water
12oz (350g) chopped almonds
½ teaspoon ground cinnamon

For the syrup
2 glasses/8oz sugar
1 glass/100ml water
juice of ½ lemon

1. Melt the butter, sugar and water in a pan and stir in the chopped nuts and spice.

2. Brush the base of a large, deep baking dish with melted butter. Layer half the sheets of filo pastry over the bottom of the dish, brushing each with melted butter.

3. Spread the nut filling over the pastry.

4. Layer the remaining sheets of filo over the filling, brushing them all with melted butter as before.

5. Brush butter over the top of the baklava and cut in diamond shapes with the point of a knife, deep enough to penetrate the top layers of the pastry.

6. Bake in a moderate oven for 40-50 minutes, or until golden brown.

7. While the baklava is baking make up the syrup by boiling the sugar, water and lemon juice together for 10 minutes. Leave it to cool.

8. Pour the cool syrup over the hot baklava as soon as it comes out of the oven.

NB. For maximum absorption, pour a cool syrup over a hot pastry or/a hot syrup over a cool pastry.

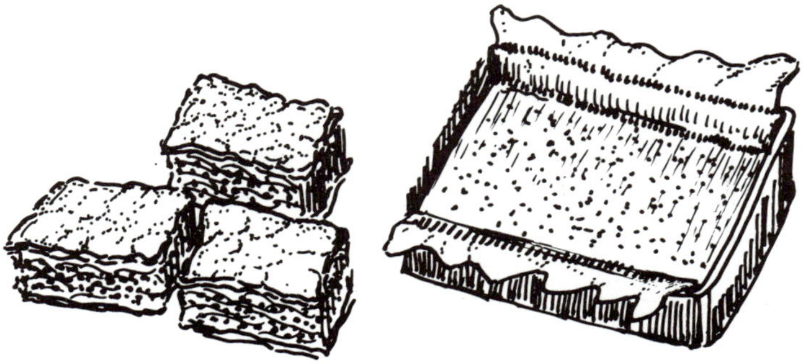

• Brandy Sour •

Touchdown in Cyprus, what excitement! As we crossed the shimmering tarmac to the air terminal, long cool drinks were very much on our minds. It wasn't long before we were sitting in the shade of a palm tree, sipping our first Brandy Sour, magic! The charm of Cyprus had enveloped us all.

Brandy sour is 'the' drink of Cyprus. It combines local brandy and the fresh tang of Cyprus lemons.

Ingredients

2 parts (50ml) brandy (Cyprus cocktail brandy is not strong)
1 part (25ml) lemon squash - as pure as possible
2 drops angostura bitters
top up with soda
add lots of ice cubes

Decorate with a slice of fresh lemon and serve immediately, with a straw, a cool breeze and a view of the sea!

• Filletaggia Hirina Sti Skhara — Pork Fillets on Charcoal •

Spring, summer, autumn or winter, whatever the season, Cypriots-like to barbecue. Not with a sophisticated table-high ornate barbecue set but crouching low, out of the wind, over a cast iron trough which is glowing red with hot coals. These grills are not as basic as they first appear, for most have a dozen steel kebab skewers as well as three larger skewers for roasting a whole leg of lamb or chicken. All these skewers rotate with the help of a small motor.

Grilled food must be tasty but tender and the Cypriots eat a great deal of home grown pork. Fillet of pork is the natural choice for flavour and texture, but if this is more extravagant than you would choose, then select lean looking loin chops.

By marinading the pork first in a combination of oil, lemon juice and herbs you can be sure of a succulent, aromatic meal, served with extra slices of lemon for those who like their meat on the sharp side.

• Serves 4 •

Ingredients

1½lbs (750g) fillet of pork

1½ large juicy lemons

1 glass (100ml) olive oil

a good handful of fresh herbs, rigani (marjoram), tyme or basil

salt and freshly ground black pepper

1. Squeeze the juice from the lemons, combine with the oil, herbs and seasoning and pour over the pork fillets in a shallow dish. Leave to marinate for at least 2 hours, longer if possible, turning from time to time.

2. Light the barbecue or preheat the grill so that it is really hot when you start to cook. Grill the pork fillets until they are crisp and brown on all sides, pouring over the marinade if they become too dry and hard.

3. Serve the fillets straight from the grill, pour over a little of the marinade to moisten them, serve with slices or chunks of fresh lemon and a sprinkling of fresh herbs.

4. A salad of cucumber, yogurt and mint **TALATOURI** served with this grill would be perfect.

• Fruit Liqueurs •

The summer months in Cyprus see a bountiful crop of fruit, but because the weather is so warm the fruit ripens very fast and doesn't last for long. One of the best ways to preserve some of the summer crop is to macerate it in alcohol and this will give you a fruity liqueur as well as some sozzled fruit to enjoy later in year.

In Cyprus the residue from the grape harvest is distilled into a heady spirit called Zivania. As a neat drink it is powerful stuff and most people recommend that you either rub it on your chest or use it to clean the windows! It does, however, make a very good fruit liqueur and sells for a song if you can find any.

Vodka, gin or brandy are all suitable alternatives.

Ingredients

Top quality fresh fruit, unblemised and not over ripe
Caster sugar
Sealable jars
Alcohol

1. Pick over fruit and and wash and dry if necessary. Half peaches and apricots and add a few cracked stones for flavour. Prick fruit like plums and sloes with a pin to help release the juices.

2. Arrange the fruit to the top of the clean and dry jars and fill up to a third of the jar with caster sugar.

3. Cover with alcohol, right up to the top.

4. Seal the jars and leave for at least a month to mature, turning from time to time to distribute the sugar.

Serve the liqueurs in small glasses and eat the fruit with ice cream, fresh cream or yogurt and some crisp biscuits.

N.B. Make sure that the fruit is completely submerged in liquid.

• Horiatiki Salata — Village Salad •

No visitor to Cyprus could have missed this delicious local peasant salad. The ingredients are hardly complicated, but the combination gives horiatiki salad a flavour of its own.

Based on fresh seasonal vegetables the Cyprus salad resembles a Greek salad of tomatoes, onions, olives and fetta cheese. But it offers much more variety. You will often find shredded white cabbage and depending on the time of year it may include **rocca,** (rocket), **glysrida** (purslane), **louvana** (the green tops of the pea plant) **koliandros** (coriander leave) and **capari** (pickled stems of the caper plant).

The dressing is very simple, pure olive oil with perhaps a squeeze of lemon juice, and it is the basic coating for all salads and hot vegetable dishes too.

In some tavernas you will find the Arab influence of chopping all the salad ingredients very small, whilst in village tavernas the salad greens aren't chopped at all, but left whole for the individual to chew like a rabbit!

One of the most haunting flavours is **koliandros** or coriander. It is a member of the parsley family, both the green leaves and the seeds are widely used in the Middle East. The flavour of the leaves is an acquired taste — the name of this pungent herb comes from the Greek koris, meaning bug, indicative of its aroma. However it is also similar to the aroma of dried orange peel, a more acceptable comparison. Koliandros is widely used in the cooking of Afghanistan, Iran, the Gulf States and the Yemen.

Ground coriander seeds are also widely used and feature in the Baharat of the Gulf States and Iraq.

• Serves 4-6 •

Ingredients

**1 small white cabbage, shredded*

a bunch of rocket, purslane, louvana, or parsley, snipped with scissors

4 spring onions, chopped

1 small or ½ large cucumber, skin on, diced

3-4 large ripe juicy tomatoes, quartered

a handful of coriander leaves

50g (2oz) fetta cheese, in slices

black olives

juice of 1 lemon

**NB. Lettuce may alternatively be used in which case instead of lemon juice use vinegar and olive oil.*

1. In a large salad bowl arrange the ingredients in the order given.

2. Add as much oil as you like, squeeze over the lemon juice and toss to mix the salad.

If there is salad left I find it makes a tasty and quick filling for pitta bread sandwiches.

• Houmous — Chick-Pea Dip •

Revithia or chick peas are a basic ingredient in Cyprus cooking. They appear in casseroles, salads, sauces, dips and even as a raising agent in a traditional village bread called **arkadena.**

Houmous is eaten all over the Middle East. The addition of tahini paste (ground sesame seeds) is an influence from the Arab countries. Houmous, with its earthy nutty flavour is tantalizingly good served with toasted pitta bread.

• Serves 6 •

Ingredients
1 glass/6oz chick-peas, picked over and soaked overnight
2 cloves garlic
2 tablespoons tahini paste
juice of 1 large lemon
4 tablespoons olive oil
about 1 glass/200 mls chick-pea cooking liquid
To garnish
1 tablespoon olive oil
chopped parlsey

1. Bring the peas to the boil and change the water.

2. Cover the peas with plenty of fresh water in a large pan and simmer till soft, about an hour, depending on their age.

3. Strain the chick-peas, keeping the liquid.

4. Liquidize the chick-peas with the remaining ingredients until you have a grainy puree. Add more liquid if necessary. It may be easier to blend the houmous in two batches.

5. Serve the houmous with a dribble of olive oil over the top and a sprinkling of chopped parsley.

• Ayrani — Iced Yogurt Drink •

This is one of those recipes that seems impossible when you first read through the ingredients, but try it, just once, and you may be surprised.

Turkish in origin, Ayrani is a most refreshing drink and quite filling too.

Ingredients

2 parts thick 'Greek style' yogurt, sheeps milk if possible

1 part iced water

salt and dried mint (optional) to taste

In a liquidizer or blender mix the yogurt and water till smooth. Flavour with salt and mint and chill till required.

• Kalamaria Yiemista — Stuffed Squid •

The greatest gastronomic memories for my six year old must be 'Squid'n'Chips' on the beach in sunny Cyprus! Crisp rings of kalamari and a plate of fresh fried chips — under the sun, by the sea, heaven!

I almost agree with her, but in reality, the kalamari were usually frozen and rather chewy.

An adult alternative is to gather some fresh baby squid from your favourite fisherman, clean then soak them in lemon juice. Drop into a light batter and fry till crisp, serve with a village salad and a brandy sour — its almost unbeatable!

This recipe for stuffed squid is rather more sophisticated. Perhaps a little time consuming the first time you try it, but definitely worthwhile. Stuffed squid can be served hot or cold as a first course or as a part of a meze.

• Serves 4-6 •

Ingredients

3lb (1½ kg) of small sized squids

juice of 1 lemon

2 tablespoons olive oil

Stuffing

4 tablespoons rice

5 tablespoons olive oil

1 large onion, finely chopped

½ glass/100ml dry white wine

4 tablespoons tomato puree dissolved in a glass of hot water

½ teaspoon dry mint

2 cloves

½ teaspoon cinnamon

salt and pepper

1. To clean the squid, pull the tentacles firmly away from the body. The head and insides of the squid should come off cleanly. Cut off the tentacles just above the head and keep them, but throw the head, etc. away. Slip the nib-like transparent bone out of the body and turn the body inside out. Rinse it under a cold running tap and rub off the pinkish membrance. Leave the body to soak in the olive oil and lemon juice while you make the stuffing.

2. Heat the oil and fry the onion gently to colour. Add the chopped tentacles and cook for another minute. Stir in the rice and cook until transparent, about three minutes. Add the wine, tomato puree and seasonings and cook until the liquid has been absorbed by the rice.

3. Fill the stuffing into the squid, leaving room in each for the rice to swell. Secure the top with a toothpick, and place the stuffed squid upright and closely packed in a deep baking dish.

4. Pour the marinade, that is the olive oil and lemon juice over the squid and enough boiling water to cover.

5. Bake in a moderate oven Gas 4, 350°F, 180°C for about 1½ hours until the squid are tender. By then the sauce should be quite thick.

6. Serve the stuffed squid warm or cold.

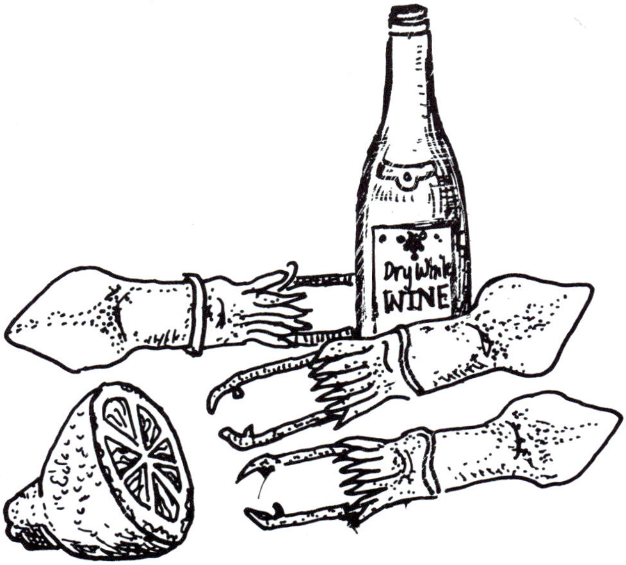

• Kleftiko •

Kleftiko comes from the verb 'to steal' in Greek, and this method of cooking is said to originate from the Greek war of Independence when groups of bandits lived in the mountains of Greece. They cooked their filched sheep or lamb with wild herbs in a sealed earthenware pot embedded on glowing embers in a hollow below the ground.

Today in Cyprus kleftiko is placed in special terracotta pots and cooked in clay ovens. They are often painted white and resemble old fashioned bee hives.

A more modern version of kleftiko is to wrap your chunks of lamb in foil together with herbs and bake in a slow oven. This is the simplest of meals to prepare, and I suggest that if you possibly can, try making kleftiko with goat meat, it is delicious!

One of the herbs to include in your kleftiko is rigani. This is wild marjoram made that little more pungent because of the hot, dry climate. It is gathered when the flowers are in bud and the herb is dried before use. Marjoram or oregano have the same flavour.

To prepare your kleftiko, ask the butcher to give you chunks of lamb, each piece with a bone in it.

Wrap your meat in a large square of foil, including in each parcel a good sprinkle of salt, some rigani and a bayleaf.

Seal the foil well and bake in a very slow oven for 2 to 3 hours.

Cooked kleftiko should literally fall off the bone, and due to the fat produced in this long slow cooking, it is a good idea to serve kleftiko with wedges of fresh lemon which help to cleanse the palate.

• Serves according to the amount of meat •

• Kohlrabi or Carrots Levantine •

All those years of boiled carrots, such preparation, and for what an indifferent end result.

Now that the Cypriots have taught me the levantine way to prepare and serve vegetables I shall never return to 'the way my mother cooked'. The simplicity of the preparation appeals to me, with just a shake of salt and squeeze of fresh lemon, these common garden vegetables become almost luxury titbits — good enough to grace any cocktail bar.

Simply buy the freshest carrots or kohlrabi you can find.

Peel with a potato peeler and slice into matchsticks for the carrot or across into circular slices for the kohlrabi.

Then sprinkle the vegetables with salt and squeeze over a freshly cut lemon! — So simple, so good.

• Lemonada •
• Homemade Lemon Squash •

Memories of Cyprus will always conjure up the magical sight of lemons actually hanging on trees. Driving through citrus groves in spring is a treat for the blossom is nothing less than intoxicating.

When the heat is getting you down make up a jug of this fresh lemon squash. Nothing could be more refreshing.

Ingredients

3 large soft juicy lemons

or 6 ripe oranges (the thin skinned variety will yield more juice)

caster sugar

To serve

iced or soda water

still of fizzy water – well iced

1. Scrub the fruit and peel thinly with a potato peeler.

2. Put the peel in a heavy based saucepan with an 1″ of cold water.

3. Heat slowly to the boil, but don't allow to boil or the flavour will be bitter.

4. Take the pan off the heat, cover and leave to cool.

5. Squeeze the juice from the fruit and pour into a jug. Add the strained peel juice and sweeten to taste with sugar.

6. Chill the fruit syrup until required then serve in tall glasses topped up with iced water or soda water and ice cubes.

• Loukoumia — Wedding Cakes •

Little shortbread cakes, dredged in icing sugar and prettily wrapped, loukoumia are the traditional cakes served at weddings.

Similar to the Ma'amoul of Lebanon and Egypt where they are prepared for the Easter feast.

Loukoumia are eaten all the year round now in Cyprus but the filling differs with the season and occasion. Bite into a Loukoumia at a wedding and you will find an almond or pistachio, but look out for a date at Christmas!

Most Cypriot cooks prefer to use vegetable oil or a light fat called spry for baking. This gives a good light texture but I miss the richness of butter, so I have adapted the recipes to suit my taste.

• Makes about 12 •

Ingredients

4 glasses/1lb plain flour

8oz (225g) unsalted butter

1 tablespoon orange blossom or rose water

2-3 tablespoons milk or water

Dates or nuts for filling

1. Sift the flour into a large mixing bowl. Rub the butter in with your fingers as you would for a crumble.

2. Add orange blossom or rose water, followed by milk or water and work the dough until it is soft and easy to shape.

3. Take a walnut sized lump of dough and shape it around either a stoned date or nut. Press the dough back into a ball shape.

4. Decorate the tops of the pastries with a fork. (This will help the icing sugar to cling when they are baked).

5. Bake in a moderately slow oven Gas 3, 325°F, 180°C for about 20-25 minutes. They shouldn't brown at all, and may still look rather soft.

6. When the loukoumia are cool dust them thickly with icing sugar.

• Mahallepi — Creamed Rice Pudding •

This pudding is prepared during the summer months in Cyprus after the rose and bitter orange flower harvest. The fragrant waters distilled from these flowers are the vital flavour for mahallepi, a dish which is loved by young and old alike.

Although I can find no trace of such a pudding amongst Greek recipes the Arabs and Turks both prepare this dish.

• Makes about 6-8 •

Ingredients

2 pints/1.2 litres milk

2 tablespoons cornflour

3 tablespoons ground rice

8 tablespoons sugar

2 tablespoons rose water or orange blossom water

2oz (50g) chopped almonds, skins on

1. Mix cornflour, ground rice and sugar to a paste with a little of the milk.

2. Bring the rest of the milk to boil and pour a little into the paste, stirring well. Transfer this back to the pan over the heat and stir hard until the mixture is smooth. (Take care not to let the milk burn on the bottom of the pan or it will flavour the mahallepi.)

3. When the mixture has thickened, take off the heat and add the rose water.

4. Leave the mahallepi to cool before pouring it into one large or 4-6 individuals bowls. Sprinkle the chopped almonds on top and serve cold.

• Melitzanosalata — Aubergine Puree Salad •

In Cyprus melitzanosalata is served as part of a meze, or with chunks of fresh bread and a long cool drink. It has an unusual and rather exotic flavour which maybe why it is called 'poor man's caviar'. To contradict this, though, I am told that this aubergine puree was invented by the ladies of the Sultan's harem — to win his favours!

Although the Cypriots call this salad melitzanosalata as do the Greeks, the addition of tahini encourages me to think that this recipe arrived with the Arabs, either from Syria, but more likely from Lebanon. Some recipes often include yogurt, you may like to try this.

• Serves 4-6 •

Ingredients

2-3 large aubergines
2 cloves garlic, crushed with salt
1 medium onion, grated (optional)
2 tablespoons tahini paste
juice of 1 large lemon
1 teaspoon paprika pepper
2-3 tablespoons olive oil

1. First burn your aubergines! To achieve the proper smokey flavour the aubergines need to be grilled, either over a barbecue or under the grill until the glossy black skin begins to burn. Finish cooking the aubergines in the oven if necessary, they must be cooked right through.

2. Peel away the skin and put the aubergine flesh into a liquidizer.

3. Now add olive oil to taste. The puree needs to taste rich but not over oily.

4. Garnish with chopped parsley and black olives.

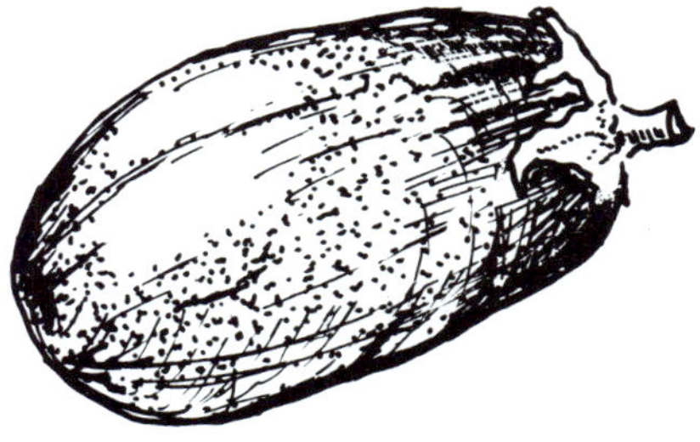

• Psari Plaki — Fish Plaki •

Fish plaki is a very popular recipe in Cyprus inherited from the Greek Islands.

The basis of all plaki recipes are lemon, garlic, olive oil, tomatoes and wine.

All sorts of fish can be cooked 'plaki'. The ingredients of the sauce enhance their own subtle flavours.

• Serves 4 •

Ingredients

2lb (1kg) fish, seabream, bass, John Dory, halibut, cod or haddock

1 large onion, sliced

1 large clove garlic, crushed

1 teaspoon ground fennel or coriander seeds

3 tablespoons olive oil

salt and black pepper

1 large lemon

1-2 tablespoons chopped parsley

14oz (425g) tin tomatoes

½ glass/100ml white wine

1. Scale, gut and clean the fish and place it whole in a oiled baking dish. Sprinkle generously with salt, freshly ground pepper and the juice from half the lemon.
2. Heat the remaining oil in a pan and fry the onion and crushed garlic over medium heat, until soft and transparent. Stir in the tomatoes, with their juices, add the parsley, crushed seeds and wine. Cook this sauce for a few minutes until well blended, then season with salt and pepper.
3. Pour the sauce over the fish, topping up with little water, if the baking dish is large. Cut the remaining lemon into thin slices and lay them on top of the fish. Cover the dish with foil or a lid, and bake in the centre of a pre-heated oven, at Gas 5, 375°F, 190°C for about 45 minutes.
4. Serve the fish in the sauce straight from the dish with potatoes or lots of fresh bread to soak up the juices.

• Sheftalia •

The day that we picked Tony and Katerina's olives was very special.

Armed with baskets and ladders we set about the large old olive trees that had belonged to the Policarpou family for generations. It wasn't so much that Katerina wanted to preserve and pickle the olives or have them pressed for her supply of olive oil, her sister had plenty for everyone, but it just wasn't right to leave them on the trees. Almost as though the trees would take anger and not produce their cherished crop again.

Picking the olives was just an excuse though — as we discovered when we arrived at the small orchard that had such a magnificent view over Episkopi village. Tony had already lit the grill and village wine was warming beside it.

We ate chunks of fresh pork that had been marinated in wine and herbs and as if that wasn't enough there were Katerina's home made sheftalia too.

These simple sausages are made from minced pork with parsley and seasonings and are wrapped in panna or caul. Panna is an elastic film marbled with fat from the lining of a sheep or pigs intestine and is available from most good butchers. It adds a delicious flavour and moisture to the sheftalia and is used in the same way by the Welsh for their faggots and the French for their crepinette sausages.

• Serves 6 •

Ingredients

1lb (450g) coarsely ground pork
1lb (450g) finely ground pork
1 large onion, grated
½ glass/4 tablespoons chopped fresh parsley
2 teaspoons salt
freshly ground black pepper
8oz (225g) panna

1. Soak the panna in water and wine vinegar for ten minutes.
2. Mix the minced porks, onion, parsley and seasoning.
3. Cut the panna into rectangles about 3″ x 7″ (7cm by 12 cm).
4. Put about a tablespoon of filling onto the panna and roll into sausage shapes.
5. Grill the sheftalia over glowing coals or grill gently so that they cook through to the middle. Sheftalia taste especially good when they are well cooked and served with a squeeze of fresh lemon inside a warmed pocket of pitta bread.

• Souvla •

High days and holidays in Cyprus are celebrated whenever possible with a barbecue in the fresh air.

No trouble with the weather since it is guaranteed dry and sunny from April to October. And since most families have portable grills which fit in the back of the car, the occasion can be celebrated in any shady glade you choose. Drive around Cape Greco on a Sunday and you will find yourself in the midst of a marvellous party. Cypriot families will have settled down amongst the untamed landscape, lit their grills and smoke will be drifting heaven-wards from fifty different gatherings. These simple barbecue sets usually have a battery operated spit which slowly rotates over the glowing embers to cook the meat consistently.

Souvla will be the order of the day. Large chunks of goat or lamb, marinated and seasoned with fresh herbs, lemon juice and salt, then threaded onto the spit, and cooked till very very tender.

• Serves 4-6 •

Ingredients

3lb (1½ k) lamb - cut into chunks, each including a piece of bone
1 glass/200ml dry red or white wine
3 tablespoons sunflower or olive oil
4 bayleaves
1 large onion, finely chopped
1 tablespoon fresh rigani, (oregano), tyme, rosemary or basil
2 teaspoons salt
freshly ground black pepper

1. Put the chunks of lamb into a large bowl and add the remaining ingredients. Mix well and leave to marinate for at least 2 hours.

2. Thread the meat onto large skewers and grill over gentle heat for about an hour, turning every 10 minutes and basting with the marinade at the same time.

3. Cooking souvla is a pastime as well as an art and everyone in the party must be encouraged to check on the well being of the roasting meat and take an interest in its preparation and cooking. In this way you can be sure that all appetites will be well whetted by the tantalising smells coming from the barbecue.

• Souvlakia Me Pitta — Kebabs in Pitta Bread •

Souvlakia or shish kebab dates back to the imperialist era of the Ottoman Empire when the soldiers on campaign ate whatever they could. Small pieces of fresh meat, skewered and grilled over an open fire became the standard battle food.

Souvlakia are popular throughout Cyprus, but pork is used more often than lamb because it is leaner and cheaper. Buying meat for souvlakia is simple in Cyprus, because most butchers sell ready cubed pork. All that remains to be done is to soak it in rough red wine for a couple of hours, together with some herbs and spices and then light the barbecue.

Pitta bread turns souvlakia into a mobile meal. No plates or cutlery necessary, just toast the pitta over the charcoal for a minute or two, split and fill them with the cooked meat, some chopped salad and a good squeeze of fresh lemon juice.

All you need to do is choose a quiet corner of the beach, garden, wood or wild hildside and wander off . . .

• Serves 4-6 •

Ingredients

2lb (1k) lean pork or lamb, cubed
enough red wine to cover meat
2 onions, quartered
2 bay leaves

To baste the souvlakia as they grill

2 tablespoons oil
juice of 1 lemon
rigani or oregano
salt

For the salad

3-4 ripe tomatoes, chopped
half a cucumber, chopped
some leaves of lettuce, shredded
2 tablespoons parsley, chopped

1. Soak the cubed meat in the wine with the chopped onion and bay leaves for at least a couple of hours.

2. Mix all the ingredients for the salad together.

3. Light the barbecue in good time so that the fiercest heat will have passed before cooking begins.

4. Thread the cubes of pork onto skewers, interspersing them with the onion and bayleaves from the marinade.

5. Grill the skewers over moderate heat, turning from time to time. When the meat is half cooked, brush over a mixture of oil and fresh lemon juice and sprinkle over some salt and herbs. Continue basting like this until the souvlakia are ready.

6. Grill the pitta bread for a few minutes before half filling each with the cooked meat. Add some salad and serve a wedge of lemon with each.

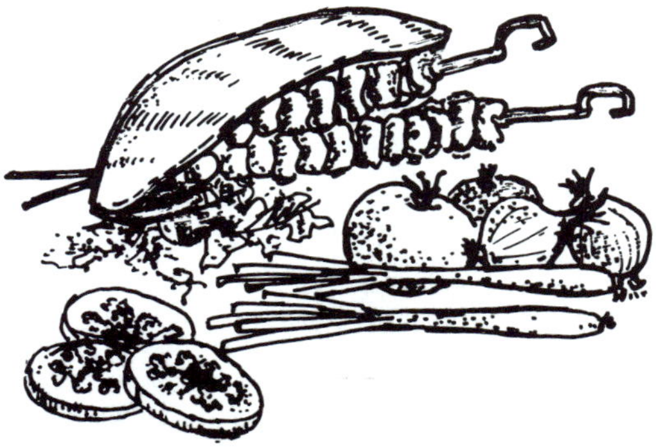

• Tahini Dip •

It is in the very nature of a Cypriot to relax. Stress is not a national characteristic! Living in Cyprus one adjusts to the eternal optimism of the people and a certain gentle ease about decision making and punctuality. Worried visitors are easily reassured by a smile and 'No problem' quoted from their hospitable hosts.

Arriving at a taverna for a meal it is natural to relax and unwind in the friendly atmosphere. Whether the menu offers what it says seems hardly to matter, perhaps there is something else on offer that day. In this easy going society though, one thing is for sure — *There will always be tahini dip!*

Tahini comes from crushed sesame seeds and is a vital ingredient in everyday diet. Eaten as a sauce, dip, salad dressing, or sweetened and spread on bread or in cakes. Who can say how it first arrived in Cyprus, since all the neighbouring countries of the Eastern Mediterranean eat Tahini too.

Tahini paste is available in jars or tins from delicatessens or large supermarkets.

• Serves 6-8 •

Ingredients

4 tablespoons tahini paste
2 cloves garlic, crushed with salt
juice of 2 lemons
4 tablespoons olive oil
1 teaspoon ground cumin seeds
cold water to thin
chopped parsley for garnish

1. Combine all the ingredients, beating hard. This is best done in a food processor.

2. Add enough cold water to give a pouring consistency.

Serve tahini with fresh bread, warm pitta bread or as a dressing for salads, grills, fish or even in sandwiches!

• Koupepia — Stuffed Vine Leaves•

Koupepia literally means little cigar — an apt description for the Cypriot version of the dolma.

Dolmas, dolmathes, dolmeh, mahshi, koupepia or stuffed vine leaves are eaten in every country of the Eastern Mediterranean. They demonstrate the essence of Middle Eastern cooking, intricate and time consuming in their preparation but the pride of a good hostess.

So diverse are the recipes for 'dolmas' that only the outer casing or vine leaf is common to all. Depending on the region they may be served hot or cold and have a variety of sauces such as tomato, egg and lemon or just olive oil. The fillings are as various, including rice, cracked wheat, minced meat, nuts, garlic, onions, dried fruit, tomatoes and various herbs and spices.

I am lucky to have a vine winding its way over my veranda. These vines are specifically planted to give maximum shade in the summer and are called percolas.

In late April or early May, just as soon as the first bright green leaves reach a good size I pluck a handful and cagoule one of the children to help me fill and roll our first koupepia. I find the sharp lemony flavour of these young vine leaves irresistible and they appear in a great many of my dishes.

The microwave is ideal for cooking koupepia. It steams them gently in their own juices and by using a glass casserole they don't collect any metallic saucepan flavours.

• Serves 4-6 •

Ingredients

20 vine leaves

50g/2oz long grain rice

1 onion, chopped

2 tablespoons olive oil

100g (4oz) minced lean lamb

2 tablespoons tomato puree

2 tablespoons chopped parsley

½ glass (100ml) water or light stock

salt and pepper

4 tablespoons olive oil and the juice of 1 lemon – for cooking

1. If you are using a packet of vine leaves, they need to be soaked in boiling water for about half an hour, then refreshed in cold water for 5 minutes. With fresh vine leaves, plunge them into boiling water for about a minute just to let them wilt, then straight into cold water.

2. Snip off the stalk and spread the leaves over a wide area ready to fill.

3. For the filling: Fry the onion in the oil until it begins to colour. Add the rice and lamb and stirfry for about 3 minutes until the rice has turned transparent and the meat lost its redness.

4. Add the tomato puree, parsley, seasoning and enough liquid to moisten. Simmer for 5 minutes. Cover and leave the filling to cool.

5. Put a teaspoonful of the filling into the centre of each vine leaf. Fold the base of the leaf over the filling then fold in the sides. Now roll up just like a cigar.

6. Cover the base of a saucepan, casserole or microwave dish with spare vine leaves. Place the koupepia carefully on top and cover the whole lot with more vine leaves. Pour over the oil and lemon juice and cook gently for about half an hour. Press a saucer down on top of the koupepia if cooking in a saucepan, it will stop them breaking up.

Serve your koupepia hot with avgolemoni (egg and lemon) sauce or cold just as they are.

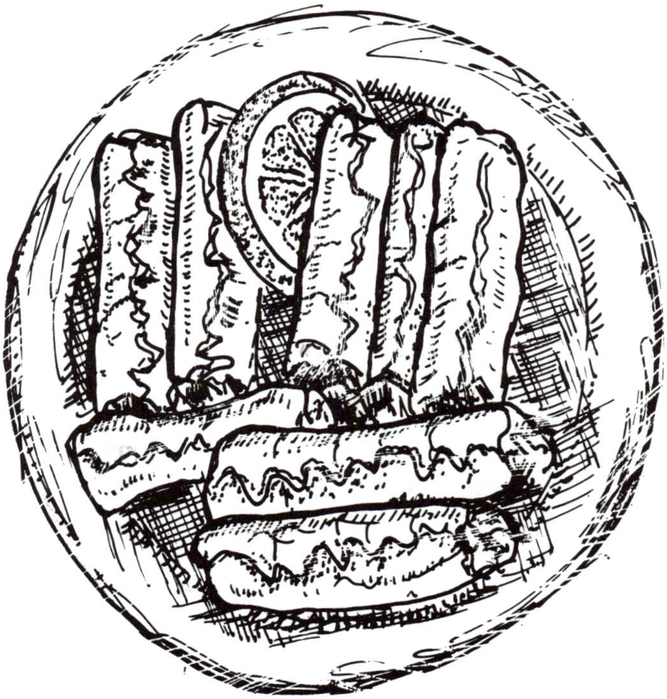

Autumn

"Work is hard, no work is harder" — *Greek Proverb*

As the heat from the summer sun softens a little and the nights draw in, so the activity in the fields and orchards reaches a crescendo. Autumn is the busiest time of the year for Cyprus' rural community as the harvest gets under way.

The delectable table grapes that refreshed us all summer long now make way for the wine grapes, which are so plump that they squeeze their juice onto the road in a steady stream from the back of the lorries.

Groups of pickers move from carob tree to carob tree. Filling their sacks, they sell most of the crop to the wholesaler but always keep enough for the family's needs during the coming winter.

Almonds begin to fall from the trees and patient people crack them for hours, with a deft movement and the right size stone.

The olive presses, which have lain dormant for nine months now buzz with activity. They will be in operation until the early spring and during the height of the harvest run for twenty four hours a day.

The market stalls groan with autumn produce. Long slim white flecked aubergines appear and pale green courgettes with their yellow trumpet flowers. These are regarded as the best varieties by the Cypriots, but don't take my word for it, taste them yourself!

Boxes and boxes of green olives arrive, to be sold quickly to housewives who want to crack and prepare them for storing over the winter months. My favourite autumn fruit, the fig, arrives in both green and purple varieties. They tempt me so much that having bought a bagful in the market I rarely have any left by the time I get home! I prefer to eat them simply with a squeeze of lemon and perhaps a nibble of salty fetta cheese.

Autumn may bring work to many but it also gives the inmates of the island a chance to celebrate. Festivals for the various crop harvests take place throughout the land.

The first and biggest is the Wine Festival.

Don't miss it if you visit Cyprus in September. Limassol hosts this ever growing 'party' and apart from tasting all the Cyprus wines you will have a chance to see traditional wine presses, taste local specialities and even join in some Cypriot dancing.

Throughout the wine producing villages on the slopes of Troodos you will find smaller festivals. Kilani, a village with the most hospitable inmates, will make you more than welcome. Taste the various wine products from sultanas to palouze, the grape pudding and even sip at Zivania, a pure spirit distilled from the pips and skins of the grapes which has a rather dehabilitating effect. Definitely a drink to experience, but maybe not in any great quantity!

Arsos is another village which proudly invites visitors to sample its village wine and it would be harder to find a better way to spend an autumn day than sipping Arsos wine in the village square there.

Lastly, Anoyira plays host to a pastelle festival and visitors are invited to taste the carob syrup spread thickly on village bread.

So, if autumn is the time you pick to visit Cyprus, you can be sure of seeing the Cypriot people at their best. Their natural charm is ever present but how hard they work, and don't they know how to celebrate.

THE GRAPE HARVEST

Gluttony! It's the only word to describe the way in which all the inhabitants of Cyprus gorge themselves on lusciously sweet table grapes during the summer. Grapes, grapes, grapes, big and juicy, small and sweet, black, white or a mixture of the two; they are all extraordinarily delicious, and as well as a good taste they give the perfect refreshment one needs to combat the fierce summer sun in July and August.

The grape harvest in Cyprus is phenomenal. It begins in June when sultanina the early pipless table grapes are picked mainly for export, and continues until November when the last of the wine grapes are gathered from the upper slopes of the Troodos mountains.

The grape crops never fails in Cyprus; it may differ in quantity from year to year but grapes are guaranteed. With such a constant and plentiful source of food on their doorstep it is not surprising that the villagers in Cyprus put their grapes to as many good uses as possible. Although every day loaded lorries leave the vineyards destined either for the docks to be exported or to the four large vineries in Limassol, there are always grapes to spare. Life can get tough in the colder winter months, so during the autumn there is much activity to make provisions for the store cupboard.

Palouze is one of these speciality dishes prepared throughout Cyprus in September and October. It is a sweet and fragrant grape puree, thickened and served with a smattering of almonds on top. The main ingredient is unfermented grape juice, which is heated in a large copper pot called a **hartchi.** Not so long ago these hartchi were heated over an ever hungry wood fire but more often these days a very large gas burner is used to maintain an even heat. To purify the hot grape juice some 'aspro-homa' which literally means white earth or as we know it, Fullers' earth is added. The sediment collects at the bottom of the pan, so that once the juice has reached boiling point the surface is skimmed and the pot left to cool. After about 10 minutes the juice is strained from the hartchi into another equally large vessel, leaving all the sediment behind.

The pure unsweetened grape juice is then returned to the hartchi and some flour blended in to thicken in the proportion of 1 glass juice to 1 tablespoon plain flour. As the juice comes to the boil it must be stirred continuously, and as it thickens some flavourings are added. These are usually cinnamon, rosewater or orange flower water and masticha which is a type of resin from the Chio pine tree and much enjoyed by the Cypriots.

Palouze served warm, straight from the pan is a real delicacy in any situation. But for a really traditional experience then visit one of the villages during the autumn when they are celebrating their wine festivals.

Drink the local wines, watch the dancing, enjoy the hospitality of the villagers and queue with hundreds of locals and visitors alike to scrape some steaming hot delicious palouze straight out of the pan!

Palouze though is not the only dish of the day and once the hartchi is half empty, lengths of string threaded with nuts are lowered into the thick mixture. As the palouze adheres to the string and nuts so the whole lengths are lifted out with forked sticks and left in the sun to dry. The string of nuts are dipped into the palouze at least three times over a period of hours and the end results of coated string hang from trees, verandas and all manner of auspicious drying rails! This nut filled, hardened palouze is called **soujouko** and resembles a rather long and knobbly stick of brown rock! It is fairly chewy and the nuts add a most welcome change of texture. With no sugar added palouze and soujouko are a healthy and additive free form of sweet. Ideal for modern tastes and guaranteed to keep the children quiet for hours!

Drive through rural parts of Cyprus during September and you are guaranteed to see raisins and sultanas drying in the sun. The favourite spots chosen by the Cypriots are lay-bys, where once the road wound round a sharp bend, but now due to reconstruction a piece of unused tarmac makes the perfect flat drying area.

Production of raisins has been subsidized recently by the Government. The grape producers are being encouraged to redirect more of their harvest towards drying grapes and send less to the wineries.

Since raisins and sultanas are simple to make this scheme suits everyone.

First, the small green sultanina grapes are collected and picked over to remove all stems and blemished fruit. After washing, the grapes are dipped into a solution of potassium carbonate or potash, water and a little olive oil. The potash helps to break down the grapes skins and allow them to dry out more quickly and the oil softens the skins.

The grapes are then laid out on long strips of matting and left to dry in the sun for about a week. They need to be turned from time to time, but apart from that, the process is complete except for packaging and delivery.

Cyprus boasts a large selection of traditional and local specialities, available from roadside stalls through the year but perhaps palouze and soujouko are amongst the most unusual and attractive.

A must for every visitor.

WINES OF CYPRUS

"He dragged me to a cafe and filled me with heavy red wine"
Lawrence Durrel in Bitter Lemons

"WARNING - GRAPE JUICE ON ROAD" So reads the sign on the Paphos to Limassol road during the grape picking season. And there is grape juice on the road, sticky and purple, it makes the tyres squelch!

For over three months the road is littered with grape laden lorries on their way to the four large wineries by the port in Limassol. The price for the grapes is set each year by the government and each vineyard is given a date when it should deliver its harvest for pressing, but to drive behind the lorries one can't help wondering if the first pressing isn't ending up on the tarmac!

One third of the population of Cyprus grows grapes, yet less than one tenth of Cypriots drink it. Lucky us, the wine imbibing part of the population, for wine in Cyprus is cheap as well as plentiful.

With a history of wine making going back to 900BC it is hardly surprising that the Cypriots know a thing or two about viticulture.

Think back to Dionysos who was the God of the vine and wine, and Aphrodite, the Goddess of love and beauty. She was so fond of wine that she helped to establish the importance of the grape crop for the very existence of the Cypriot nation.

Cyprus wine was considered to be so delectable that the Pharoahs of Egypt consumed it, and its fine quality did not go un-noticed by the ancient Greeks and Romans.

The discovery of two enormous wine cellars dating back to the sixth century BC at the Vouni Palace in the north west of the Island give credibility to the importance of wine for so many centuries. The first vines grown in madeira were from Cypriot stock and madeira resembles the most famous Cyprus wine — **Commandaria.**

Why should wine making come so easily to Cyprus? Is it the stable and predictable climate with long, hot sunny summers to ripen the grapes? Perhaps it is the quality of the indigenous grapes, unknown outside the Island? Is it the rich soil, volcanic in parts or can it be the wealth of knowledge that 4,000 years experience brings? Surely the answer must be a combination of all of these factors.

Alas the Cypriots have become so good at producing wine they are now making too much of it and over the past 30 years the Government has made the marketing of its wine as a top priority.

So watch out wine lovers for the changing taste of Cyprus wines. The fruits of many years of intensive study are emerging on to the market and should be carefully scrutinised over the next decade.

Out go the Pitharia. Those enormous terracotta jars that have been the home for fermenting grapes and wine maturing since 100BC. They attractively litter the Cyprus countryside and are still used for the limited production of village wine, as well as storing olive oil, wheat and honey.

Wine is made very differently now. The vast majority of grapes from the Island are processed by four large ultra modern wine producing companies in Limassol, on the south coast of the island. Experts in oenology monitor the progress of the grapes from the first pressing up to the ageing of the bottled wines in isothermic cellars. By fermenting the grapes in a controlled and cool environment the activity is kept low in order to conserve the maximum fruity flavour and aroma. The resulting wine is then decanted several times and after fining it undergoes the chilled stabilizing process in order to avoid haze during ageing in the bottle. Now that the wine making process has become so technically refined, what progress is being made on developing new grape varieties?

Up until 1958 there were only two main wine producing grapes grown in Cyprus. These are the drought resistant black mavro and the white Xynisteri, both being unique to Cyprus. Two other red varieties are Ophalmon and Lefkada which have a smaller yield but delicate flavour and deep colour. In the desire to add new flavours to Cypriot wines the Government imported some 75 new varieties. After four years in quarantine (to make sure that Cyprus remains phylloxera free) 16 were selected to integrate with the indigenous vines. The growth of these were carefully monitored and new rules for the wine industry were drawn up.

Vines for wine were restricted to plantations between 1,000 and 3,000ft. None of the ancient indigenous Mavro vines have been grown since 1981 and all vine growers are encouraged with cash incentives to re-plant their vineyards with the new varieties of grapes. These new vines must be planted farther apart to allow for soil clearance and ease of harvesting and some selected areas have been established for higher quality produce.

Among the new grapes to be introduced to Cyprus soil are Cabernet Sauvignon, Cabernet Franc, Merlot, Grenach and Carignan for the reds, and Sauvignon, Semillon, Ugni blanc and Italian Malvasias for white wine.

At Zakaki on the outskirts of Limassol the Government Model Winery monitors the new variety of grapes and offers encouragement and expertise to all wine producers whether at the hobby stage, cottage industry or large commercial wine factories.

A collection of highly qualified oenologists with experience of wine making from France, Germany, Spain, USA and Australia monitor the new varieties.

By keeping thorough records of the grapes grown in different regions of the Island and under various conditions, soils and altitudes, an idea of the new wines in the pipeline are now coming to light.

But there are breakaway groups of wine producers who are practising wine making on a smaller scale.

One of these is the Khrysorroyiatissa Monastery in Pano Panayia on the edge of the Paphos forest. Here some fine wines have been produced recently under the watchful eye of the Bishop.

Lastly, just to confuse the wine issue in Cyprus, it appears to have gone full circle. Wine is again being made in village co-operatives, just as it was in the beginning. But the new village wineries have the advantage of all that has gone before them. They may be a little more expensive but no one can say that they lack individual character!

So watch out for the Cyprus labels on bottles of wine you purchase and sip your wine with a greater degree of discrimination. Remember that in Cyprus there is now a new development in the bond between the expertise of a history of viticulture and the flavour of new types of grapes.

Whether you choose a wine produced from a single grape or a blended wine from a variety of grapes, be alert and see if you can't taste the sunshine under which the vines ripened.

So Cheers, *stin iyia sou,* skol, here's to you . . . the wine industry in Cyprus is definitely looking Rosé!

THE CAROB HARVEST

"The hardest crusts always fall to the toothless"

Greek Proverb

From about mid summer the long slim dark pods fall from the carob tree and humans and animals alike pounce on them for a sweet snack. Just snap a carob pod and suck the sticky sweet syrup that will immediately begin to trickle out.

Carobs are one of the largest crops grown in Cyprus, annually about 300,000 kilos. They are gathered with enthusiasm since the recent interest in carob as a chocolate substitute has pushed the price up, but they have always been an important crop, since the time of Christ.

Sometimes known as St. John's Bread, carobs were the main diet for John the Baptist in the wilderness. The carob is also called the locust bean — were these the wild locusts that John ate?

Picking starts around 24th August and individuals, families, and small factories gather their carobs from trees all over the island. You may purchase a property on the island but the carob tree in your garden could belong to someone else — and the owner will be along pretty soon to gather his crop!

Did you know that the carob seed is the original carat — goldsmiths used it as a measure for their gold.

The seed is still the most valuable part of the pod and is used in the production of cosmetics. In Cyprus the majority of pods are used as animal fodder but there are two other traditional products. The first is **Teratsomelo,** a carob syrup which is made by pouring boiling water over baskets full of broken carob pods. This liquid is then boiled until thick and the dark brown liquid, often referred to as carob honey, is sold for 75 cents a bottle. It makes a refreshing drink added to iced water or milk, but beware, for it is the perfect antidote for constipation!

The other delicacy produced from the carob syrup is **Pastelli.** The villagers first prepare teratsomelo and continue to boil it over a number of days very slowly in a big pot over the ashes of a fire. It needs to be stirred constantly with a wooden paddle until it becomes sticky and begins to change colour. It is then tipped out onto a wet surface and cut into pieces. These are thrown against a wall and pulled out again and again, a process very similar to that suffered by our Brighton rock. The Pastelli thickens and turns a beautiful golden colour, rather like the inside of a crunchy bar. It is cut into fingers and sold for 25 cents for a 100g piece. Look out for it in the markets or village shops, particularly during the winter.

Anoyira, a pretty village situated in the hills above Evdimou, between Paphos and Episkopi is at the centre of the carob growing region. Every autumn the villagers of Anoyira hold a pastelli festival and visitors are welcomed to a feast of fun. Stout cheerful ladies, clad in black, take it in turns to stir the foaming golden sweet pastelli syrup. Visitors are given a slice of village bread and encouraged to dip it into the molten mass. As the pastelli cools and hardens it turns into a very chewy bite and many visitors are silenced for some time!

The police station, conveniently situated in the centre of the village houses a make-shift kitchen and everyone queues to collect a plate of food. As with most festivals, the Cypriots really push the boat out and for just a handful of cents you will be given a plate groaning with seasonal specialities. Large chunks of roast lamb or goat, some salad, a wedge of pasticcio and perhaps a spoonful of ressi, the lamb and wheat stew always served at family celebrations.

Taking your plate and a glass of village wine it is wise to head for a tent and settle down to enjoy your meal before the dancing begins.

ELIES — OLIVES

We sat in the autumn sunshine, with baskets at our feet, the glowing coals cooking our sheftalia, and a glass of Palehouri wine in our black stained hands.

How we enjoyed that day, picking olives is one of the greatest pleasures we have experienced in Cyprus. Katerina was more than surprised at our enthusiasm for gathering their olive crop, *'You really want to pick our olives'* she said, recalling olive picking as a chore of childhood. Yes we did, and the children laughed as their fingers turned from purple to black and the smoke from the grill got into our eyes, clothes and hair.

For months and months, since late summer, Cypriots had been gathering their olives. Some picked them green and others left them to ripen to a glossy purple on the trees.

A visit to any of the olive presses would introduce you to the huge variety of olives grown on the Island. These presses hum with activity from October onwards, still in business in early February. Some presses are highly modern with stone sorting devices, heating elements and centrifugal drums which extract a far greater quantity of oil from the olives, while the older oil presses work in a fashion that can't have changed in the last thousand years. No smart machinery here, just a huge stone which rotates in a trough to break down the olives. The olives are then scooped into mesh baskets and these are stacked on top of each other under the hand press. As the olives are squeezed so the thick golden/green oil trickles through a Heath Robinson assortment of pipes and finally into bottles and jars at the other side of the room.

On the whole each olive grower uses his entire crop for home consumption. He brines and bottles the olives he and his family will need for the year and presses the rest. The oil he gathers will only just be enough for the kitchen and there is rarely any to spare. If there is he sells it at the press direct to the Olive Oil Co-operative and it is blended and sold on the island.

Olives are vital to a Cypriot's well being. Eaten for breakfast almost every day of the year, they are also found in bread and rolls for lunch and dinner! As an appetizer they appear both black and cracked green varieties, and often they find their way into cooked dishes too. The oil dresses almost every vegetable dish, hot or cold and no pulse dish survives without ladles of olive oil.

During lent olives are both cheap and nutritious and an important part of the fasting diet.

At the monastery of Khrysorroyiatissa north of Paphos, every visitor receives a traditional offering of a loaf of bread, a bottle of wine and of course, a bowl of olives. Self sufficient in every way, the monastery produces all these vitals from their land and has done so since it was first founded by a monk named Ignition in 1152.

Olives have been grown in the Mediterranean area since the Neolithic Age. Looking at enormous, silver grey gnarled olive trees one can easily believe them to be over 300 years old. They only begin to bear fruit from their sixth or seventh year, but do not reach their full yield, some twenty to forty kilos until about twenty five years. The olives are harvested every year, but some trees produce only every other year.

There are over sixty different varieties of olives grown in the world, in Cyprus though the indigenous variety suits the locals best. Olives from Spain which have a high oil yield have recently been introduced as have some of the large Greek varieties such as Amphicis and Galamon.

AMIGDALA — ALMONDS

The almond is probably the world's most popular nut. It has been grown in Cyprus since the Romans ruled this part of their Empire. Nuts are used in so many Middle Eastern dishes — for sauces, in savoury dishes, sweet puddings and of course the wonderful syrup dripping pastries.

One of the prettiest sights during spring in Cyprus are the orchards on the lower slopes of Troodos quite pink with almond blossom.

By mid summer the almonds have split their outer hulls and are ripe for picking but they will stay safely on the tree until the first autumn rains. For this reason many families pick their almonds over quite a few weeks.

Many of the almonds grown in Cyprus are an indigenous variety which thrive on the dry climate and lack of irrigation, but many new varieties have also been introduced recently from Spain, France and Italy.

Neighbouring countries use walnuts, pine nuts and pistachio nuts in their cuisine, however, in Cyprus, nothing is rated more highly than their Amigdala.

• Afelia •

Afelia is to Cyprus what steak and kidney is to Britain. It is a simple stew of pork, red wine and crushed coriander seeds.

Pork in Cyprus is plentiful and always sold extremely fresh. The price of about £1 a kilo is subsidized by the Government and so it's not surprising that more pork is eaten here than any other meat.

Coriander, (koliandros) which is the main flavouring for afelia is a spice that is essential to the Cypriot kitchen and is also used throughout the arab world.

Coriander is used as a crushed seed and also as leaf for salads and garnish. It is a member of the parsley family and the pungent flavour of the leaves is quite different from the gently slightly musty orange taste of the ground seeds. The name coriander comes from the Greek *koris,* meaning bug, (do the coriander leaves really smell so bad?)

• Serves 4-6 •

Ingredients

2lb (1k) boneless lean pork, diced

1 glass/200ml red wine

1-2 tablespoons coriander seeds, crushed coarsely

salt and lots of freshly ground black pepper

1 stick cinnamon

6 tablespoons sunflower or vegetable oil

1. Marinade the meat in the wine and spices for at least 4 hours, overnight if possible.

2. Lift the meat out of the marinade and dry on kitchen paper. Keep the marinade for later.

3. Heat the oil in a heavy based casserole and brown the cubes of meat, a few at a time, until all are crisp and brown. Add more oil if necessary.

4. Wipe any excess oil from the pan and return all the meat, pour over the marinade and enough cold water to just cover the meat. Cover the casserole with a lid and cook gently, either in the oven or on top for about 30 minutes or until the meat is tender.

5. Almost all of the liquid should have evaporated to leave a thick sauce, if necessary cook the afelia uncovered for a further 10 minutes to reduce excess liquid.

NB. Afelia tastes particularly good when served with pourgouri pilafi and a salad.

• Galatoboureko or Bogatza •

Ritza appeared from the car carrying the most enormous dish of Bogatza. *'Oh it's nothing'*, she said, *'I was cooking this afternoon and I thought you might like to try a Cypriot speciality'*.

How we enjoyed Ritza's bogatza, a dish designed to suit the British palate. The middle consists of a delicately flavoured blancmange sandwiched between layers of the finest crisp filo pastry.

• Makes around 12 •

Ingredients

1lb (450g) filo pastry

6oz/180g unsalted butter, melted

For the filling

4 tablespoons ground rice

4 tablespoons cornflour

2½ pints (1½ litres) milk

5 tablespoons sugar

2 tablespoon rose or orange flower water

For the syrup

2 glasses/200g sugar

1½ glasses (300ml) water

juice ½ lemon

1-2 tablespoons rose or orange flower water

1. First make the cream filling: Mix the ground rice, cornflour and sugar to a paste with a little of the milk. Heat the rest of the milk to boil.

2. Pour a little hot milk onto the paste, stir well then pour it all back into the pan. Stir continuously until the cream is smooth. (Take care not to let it burn on the bottom or it will flavour the mixture).

3. Take the pan off the heat and add the flower water.

4. Take half of the filo pastry and crush it between your fingers into the bottom of a large deep baking dish. Pour over half of the melted butter.

5. Pour the cream filling on top of the buttered pastry and with the remaining filo, also broken into flakes.

6. Pour over the remainder of the butter and bake in a moderate oven for 45 minutes, turning the heat up towards the end if the pastry needs to brown a little more.

7. Prepare the syrup as soon as the pastry is in the oven so that it has time to cool. Boil the sugar, water and lemon juice for 10 minutes. Add the flower water and leave the syrup to cool.

8. To serve, pour the syrup over the Galatoboureko and cut into wedges.

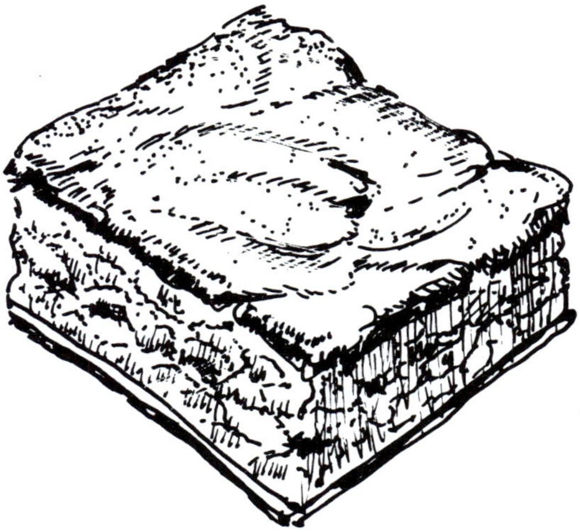

• Bourekia Me Anari – Cream Cheese Puffs •

It became apparent that Tassos was in cahoots with the fish taverna owner and within minutes of our arrival a selection of unusual dips were brought to the table.

Again, without even a peep at menu, the most varied selection of fresh fish followed, together with a simple but beautifully prepared salad. This surprise meal came to a close with yet another exquisite speciality of Cyprus, tiny deep fried pastries filled with honey and spice flavoured cheese. 'Efharisto' Tassos, thanks for a meal we won't forget in a hurry!

• Makes over 12 •

Ingredients

Pastry

3 glasses/12oz plain flour

pinch of salt

2 tablespoons sunflower oil

about 6 tablespoons lukewarm water

Cheese filling

1½ glasses/6oz fresh anari, ricotta, curd cheese or sieved cottage cheese

1-2 tablespoons runny honey

1 egg, lightly beaten

1½ teaspoons ground cinnamon

To finish

2 tablespoons orange flower water diluted with 2 tablespoons water

icing sugar

1. Sift flour and salt into a mixing bowl. Pour in oil and using fingertips, rub oil evenly into flour. Mix to a soft dough with the water, knead well until very smooth, cover and leave to rest for 1 hour.

2. Cream the cheese with honey, egg and spice.

3. Roll out the pastry as thinly as possible and cut into 3″ (8cm) circles.

4. Put a teaspoon of cheese filling in the centre of each pastry disc, moisten the edge with water, fold over and press edge with a fork to seal. Place finished pastries on a clean cloth.

5. Heat oil to 375°F (190°C) or until a cube of bread turns golden in 30 seconds. Fry pastries a few at a time, turning to brown evenly — they should cook in about 2 minutes. Lift out with a slotted spoon and drain on paper towels.

6. Serve the bourekia warm, sprinkled with orange flower water and icing sugar.

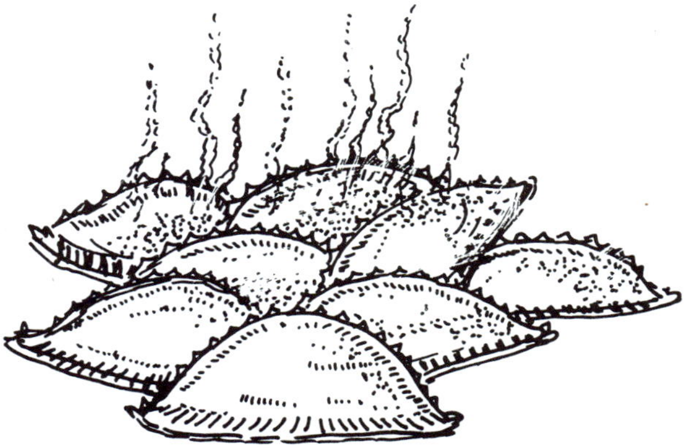

• Carob Fudge •

Although the carob crop is vast in Cyprus, carob powder has only recently become available in Cypriot shops.

Here is a quick and easy recipe using this healthy chocolate substitute, it is not a traditional idea but something that the modern Cypriot student might learn at school.

Ingredients

4oz (100g) sesame seeds
2oz (50g) carob powder
1 dessertspoon honey
few drops of vanilla essence
juice of ½ orange

1. Using a pestle and mortar or food processor, grind the sesame seeds.
2. Add the other ingredients and mix well, ideally in the food processor.
3. Form the mixture into little balls.
4. Chill well and serve in petit-four cases.

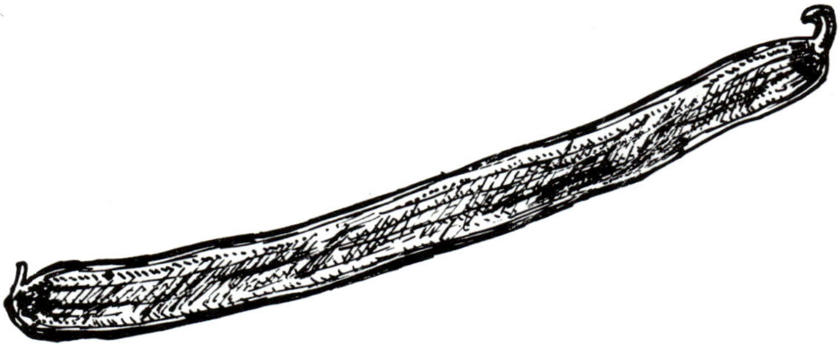

• Elies Tsakistes — Cracked Green Olives •

The Cyprus speciality for which it is famous world wide must be cracked green olives.

A bowl or saucer of these sharp, highly flavoured olives will arrive just as soon as you settle at a table in the shade, in any taverna in Cyprus.

If you don't have the chance to gather some green olives I suggest that you buy some already prepared in brine and serve them in the Cypriot sauce.

Ingredients

Fresh green olives
salt
vine leaves
lemon slices
For serving
juice of 1 lemon
1 clove garlic, crushed
2 tablespoons coriander seeds, crushed
8 tablespoons best quality olive oil

1. First find yourself a comfortable seat in the shade and find a smooth stone weighing about 1 pound or ½ kilo. Tap each olive so that the flesh cracks but not to the extent of breaking the stone.

2. Put the cracked olives in a large jar and cover with cold water. You may need to put a plate on top to ensure that they are all submerged.

3. Change the water every 24 hours; do this 4 times in all.

4. Measure the last amount of water poured from the olives before discarding. Now measure the same amount of fresh water into a large pot and add ⅓ cup of salt to each 4 cups of water. Stir over low heat until dissolved. (When cool you can check the strength of the brine with a fresh egg. The right strength is reached when the egg floats).

5. Pour the brine over the olives, place washed grape vine leaves and lemon slices on top and seal. (Some people pour a thin layer of olive oil over the surface to prevent air penetrating). Leave the olives in a dark, cool place for at least 3 weeks. They will be fine for up to a year.

6. When you want to serve the olives take out a cupful and check that they are still firm. Discard any soft ones. Rinse them under cold water, drain well and place in a bowl. Squeeze on the lemon juice, add garlic, coriander seeds and oil. Stir well and leave for a couple of hours to marinate before serving.

• Soupies Yachni — Cuttlefish Yachni •

We sat in the autumn sunshine overlooking the tiny harbour in the fishing village of Perena just a couple of miles from Cape Greco on the extreme east of Cyprus. It was Sunday morning and the tiny peninsula was deserted.

The fish taverna tempted us with its offer of fresh fish. Octopus, squids and soupies read their menu! Luckily their cooking was better than their English and we were not disappointed with our soupies yachni.

• Serves 4-6 •

Ingredients

2lb (1kg) small cuttlefish
2 large onions, sliced
1 glass/200ml olive oil
1 glass white wine
1 glass hot water
2 bayleaves
4 tablespoons chopped parsley
salt and pepper

1. Be Brave! Grasp the head and tentacles of the cuttlefish with one hand and the body in the other. Pull firmly and the two parts will separate. Discard the head but keep the tentacles. Take the chalky oval bone out of the body and rinse away everything else apart from the inksacks (silvery bags) to cook.

Wash the body and tentacles very well, remove all traces of sand and chop into smallish pieces.

2. Heat the oil in a frying pan, cook the onions till golden then add the cuttlefish and let them colour too.

3. Add the wine, water, herbs seasoning and the inksacks. Cover and bring to the boil and cook gently until almost all the liquid has evaporated.

• Hirino Me Melitzanes — Pork with Aubergines •

"So long as he has a tooth left a fox won't be pious"

Greek proverb.

This is a classic Cypriot dish. Pork is good and inexpensive on the island and big glossy purple aubergines now grow the year round.

• Serves 4-6 •

Ingredients

2lb (1k) lean pork, cubed
1 large onion, chopped
1 clove garlic, crushed
4 tablespoons sunflower oil
4 large ripe tomatoes, grated or 1 big tin tomatoes in juice
salt and freshly ground black pepper
2 medium sized aubergines
1 tablespoon plain yogurt
1 tablespoon chopped parsley

1. Heat 2 tablespoons of the oil in a heavy based casserole and fry the pork briskly to brown it on all sides. This may need to be done in three or four batches.

2. Remove the pork and fry the onion and garlic in the casserole. Add the tomatoes and seasoning and then replace the pork cubes.

3. Cover the casserole and cook in a medium oven for about an hour.

4. Meanwhile slice the aubergines, sprinkle them with salt and leave for half an hour. Then wash and pat them dry with kitchen paper.

5. Fry the aubergines in the remaining oil until brown on both sides.

6. Skim fat from the casserole, arrange the aubergine slices on top, replace the lid and return to the oven for another 45 mins.

7. Serve the pork and aubergine casserole with a spoonful of yogurt spread over the surface and parsley sprinkled over the top. Warm bread or baked potatoes are all you need to serve with this dish and perhaps a mixed salad.

• Imam Bayaldi •

Credit for this famous dish must go entirely to the Turks. The title means literally *'the imam fainted'*.

But why should the Turkish priest, the imam faint? Was it because he enjoyed the dish so much that he fainted with delight and possibly over-indulgence, or was he horror-struck by the costly amount of olive oil used in the preparation of the dish!

Don't worry, your health will not be impaired by this dish, or your purse! Aubergines are no longer a luxury ingredient, and can be bought for a reasonable price, and the olive oil can be substituted by a less expensive oil such as sunflower.

Cypriot housewives often wait until the long thin purple and white flecked aubergines come into the market to make imam bayaldi. They have a mild sweet flavour and appear at the same time as the tomato glut in the autumn.

• Serves 4 •

Ingredients

4 medium sized long aubergines

salt

½ glass/100ml olive oil

2 large onions, sliced

3 cloves garlic, crushed with salt

3 large tomatoes, grated

4 tablespoons chopped parsley

1 teaspoon rigani, marjoram or oregano

freshly ground black pepper

juice of 1 lemon

1. Cut the aubergines in half lengthways. Score the flesh with a sharp knife, taking care not to pierce the outer skin. Sprinkle salt over the cut surface and leave to drain for half an hour.

2. Heat 3 tablespoons of oil in a frying pan and fry the onions gently until soft and golden. Add the garlic and then grate the tomatoes straight into the pan. Season with parsley, rigani and pepper. Let this mixture simmer gently for about 10 minutes. Leave in a bowl to cool.

3. Rinse the aubergines, squeeze and pat dry to remove excess moisture. Heat 3 tablespoons of oil and fry the aubergines on all sides until just beginning to brown. Lay them side by side in a snug fitting casserole.

4. Spoon over the tomato sauce, filling it into the aubergines if possible.

5. Mix the remaining oil with ½ a glass of warm water and the lemon juice. Pour this into the dish and cover. Cook gently for about ½ hour or until the juices have thickened and the aubergines are soft.

6. Serve the imam bayaldi straight from the casserole, or better still, leave till cool and serve as a first course or part of a mezé.

• Kateyfi •

The basic pastry dough for kateyfi is made from flour and water which is shredded like very fine wool. It used to be sold fresh, by the kilo from street vendors in Cyprus, but nowadays many people find it easier to buy it frozen from supermarkets.

Kateyfi is prepared all over Europe as well as the Middle East and you can find these sticky 'Shredded Wheat' pastries on all continental confectionery counters. Why make it yourself, you may ask, but remember that homemade Kateyfi is just as sweet as you like and the filling and fat will be of the best quality.

I like to think of warmed honey being drizzled over the Cypriot pastries, since there are bee boxes (Cypriot bee hives) all over the island. Alas, the Cypriots are particularly dependent on sugar ever since the Lusignans established sugar refineries from Kolossi to Kato Paphos in the thirteenth century. Sugar production was a great source of income until the discovery of the New World.

In Cyprus almonds are the traditional nuts used in the filling, but travel the Middle East if you like and use chopped walnuts or pistachios.

Xenia, whose mother-in-law comes from the Lebanon, tells me that spreading melted butter rather than oil over the kateyfi makes it crisp and that is how the Lebanese prefer it.

• Makes over 12 •

Ingredients

1lb (½ kilo) kateyfi pastry strands

5oz (150g) melted butter

For the filling

8oz (250g) almonds, skins on, chopped

2 tablespoons sugar

1 teaspoon ground cinnamon

1 tablespoon orange flower water

2 tablespoons water

For the syrup

2 glasses/8oz sugar

1½ glass/300ml water

1 tablespoon orange flower water

a little grated lemon rind

1. Combine all the ingredients for the syrup in a saucepan and boil gently for 5 minutes. Leave to cool.

2. Mix the ingredients for the filling together.

3. Pull off a handful of strands from the pastry and flatten on the table. Wrap them over a teaspoonful of filling, tucking the ends and edges in, so that you end up with a cigar shape.

4. Place the kateyfi into a greased baking sheet, and sprinkle the melted butter over the top.

5. Bake the kateyfi for 30 minutes in a moderate oven, until crisp and golden.

6. Pour the cooled syrup over the hot kateyfi in the dish and leave, covered for half an hour to soak.

Transfer to a clean dish to serve.

A glass of water is necessary to help wash down these sweet pastries and I think a spoonful of yogurt goes well too.

• Kaloprama — Almond and Semolina Pudding •

Translate kaloprama and you get 'good thing' which is exactly what this almond pudding is!

This moist semolina and almond cake also appears under the name shamali, revani or basbousa depending on where you eat it in the Middle East. Halva is yet another and possibly the most universal name for kaloprama but don't confuse it with the sweet sesame paste that is sold during lent and other fasting periods of the year. Halva simply means 'sweet'.

Tony, who first introduced me to the delightful name for this recipe, remembers how as a child he used to rush out of Episkopi village school at break-time to buy a slice of kaloprama, warm from the oven and dripping in syrup. He smiled as he recalled how the slices without almonds on top were always left to late-comers!

• Makes over 12 •

Ingredients

4oz (100g) butter
4oz (100g) caster sugar
grated rind of 1 lemon
3 eggs
2 glasses/8oz semolina
1 glass/4oz plain flour
3 teaspoons baking powder
½ glass/100ml milk
½ glass/2oz finely chopped, toasted almonds
blanched split almonds

For the syrup

2½ glasses/500mls caster sugar
3 glasses/600mls water
2 tablespoons lemon juice

1. First make up the syrup. Dissolve sugar in the water over heat, add lemon juice and bring to the boil. Simmer gently for 10 minutes, then leave to cool.

2. Cream butter, sugar and lemon rind until light and fluffy. Add eggs one at a time and beat in well.

3. Fold in flour, semolina and baking powder alternatively with the milk.

4. Stir in chopped nuts.

5. Spread the mixture into a butter baking tray 18 x 28 cm. (7 x 11 inch). Arrange split almonds in rows on top.

6. Bake in a moderate oven for 50 minutes until cake is golden and shrinks slightly from sides of tin.

7. When cake is cooked, pour cooled syrup over hot cake. (Syrup penetrates more evenly if cake surface is pricked with a fine skewer before pouring on syrup).

8. Leave in tin until cool, then cut into squares or diamond shapes for serving.

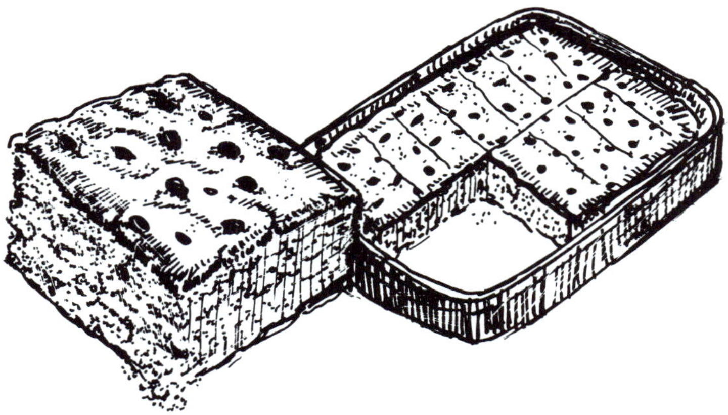

• Keftedes — Meat Balls•

These tasty little meatballs are very Greek, or perhaps simply Middle Eastern. They might pass under the name of kibbi, koukla, kibbeh, kofta, kofte or koftesi. They are a must for any meze. Fresh herbs are vital to keftedes and in Cyprus parsley is the favourite.

Parsley, so they say, absorbs fumes of wine and delays intoxication, in fact Greeks used to garland their foreheads with wreaths of parsley before embarking on a heavy drinking bout.

'Pork makes your keftedes soft' was the advice given to me, yet pork is not used by other Middle Eastern countries, even in Greece where they prefer to use lamb.

"My mother made the best keftedes before mincing machines were invented. She used to mince the pork using two sharp knives — this meant large chunks of delicious pork instead of the mince which sometimes you can hardly taste!" says Yiota!.

• Serves 4-6 •

Ingredients

2lb (1 kilo) minced pork
2 good sized potatoes, grated
1 onion, grated
1 egg
1 stick of cinnamon crushed or 1 teaspoon powdered cinnamon
a dash of grated nutmeg
salt and pepper
a little olive oil
2 tablespoons freshly chopped parsley
½ tablespoon chopped mint (optional)

1. Mix all the ingredients together, kneading well. Put the mixture in a bowl and press a crust of bread down on top to absorb any excess moisture. Leave in the fridge for at least half an hour.

2. With damp hands, roll the meat into balls of about 1″ 25cm.

3. Fry the keftedes slowly in light oil, sunflower, vegetable or soya turning from time to time. They will take about 10 minutes to cook right through.

4. Serve the keftedes hot from the pan with a crisp salad.

No Cypriot table would be without a tub of fresh yogurt and quarters of fresh lemon. Two tangy ingredients that help to 'melt' away the fat and leave you with a fresh taste on the tongue.

• Kotopoulo Elenis — Eleni's Chicken •

"The fox in her sleep dreams always of chickens"

Greek proverb

Who Eleni was I don't know, but her combination of fresh chicken, jerusalem artichokes, dill and tomatoes is very good. A dish worthy of any family gathering especially when the chicken is fresh, plump and full of flavour as they are in Cyprus.

• Serves 4 •

Ingredients

1 fresh chicken, quartered
4 tablespoons olive or sunflower oil
1 medium onion, sliced
2lb (1k) jerusalem artichokes, scrubbed clean
1 tablespoon fresh dill or ½ tablespoon dried dill
1 tablespoon tomato puree dissolved in ½ glass (100ml) water
1lb (450g) ripe tomatoes, grated or 1 large tin tomatoes in juice
salt and pepper

1. Heat the oil in a casserole and brown the chicken pieces all over, then take them out.

2. Fry the onion and whole artichokes gently for 5 minutes then add the dill, tomato puree, tomatoes and another glass of water or the juice from the tin.

3. Replace the chicken pieces, season well with salt and pepper and simmer, covered for about 45 minutes or until the chicken is cooked.

4. Serve the Chicken Eleni with pourgouri pilafi and a bowl of plain yogurt spiced with paprika.

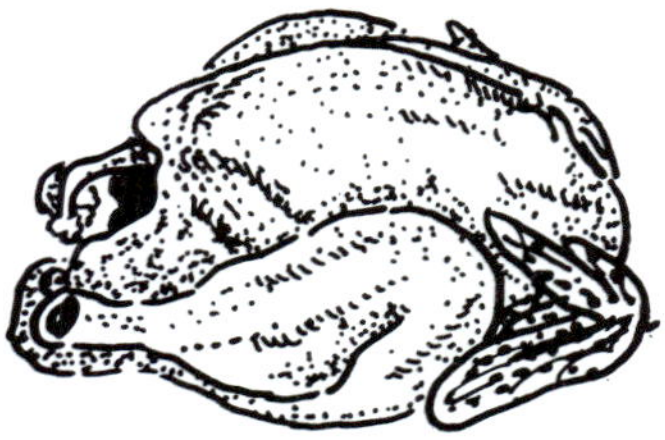

• Koupes — Cracked Wheat Cigars with a Meat Filling •

Koupes means cigar and describes accurately the appearance of these moorish meaty bites with a crisp brown coating.

There is a man in Episkopi who sells koupes every lunchtime. He wanders up and down the street with a plate of steaming temptation and a fresh lemon in his pocket for customers to squeeze over their koupes. Until a few years ago he made shirts but since he started to sell his wife's koupes . . . well, business has never looked better! Clever of the Cypriots to dream up such a dish you may say, but of course the Cyprus Koupa is just a very close cousin of the national dish of Syria and the Lebanon, the Kibbeh.

The koupa is not a simple thing to prepare and Cypriots smile in that knowing way when I despair over my lack of koupa making skill. 'There is a machine' they tell me kindly, but truthfully wouldn't dream of using it themselves!

The art of koupa making is to pound your cracked wheat until it's a soft, malleable paste and then shape it into a cigar with wet hands. With your longest finger, make a hollow down the centre of the paste and into this fill your meat mixture. Simple!

Syrian women are said to be endowed by the gods if they have a long finger favoured for the making of these kibbeh.

If you, like me, spend frustrating hours of non-achievement, then I suggest that you make a Tray Kibbeh. The ingredients are the same but the end product is cooked in a tray, rather like a baklava and takes a great deal less time to prepare!

• Makes over 12 •

Ingredients

For the paste

1lb (½ kilo) fine cracked wheat (pourgouri)

2 teaspoons salt

1½ glasses/½ pint hot water

For the filling

1lb (½ kilo) ground beef or lamb

1 tablespoon olive oil

1 large onion, sliced

1 clove garlic, crushed

4 tablespoons parsley, chopped

2oz (50g) pinenuts (optional)

salt and pepper

1. Pour the hot water over the pourgouri, add the salt and leave for a couple of hours.

2. For the filling: heat the oil and brown the meat, stirring well to break up. Add the onion and garlic and cook till soft. Stir in the parsley, nuts and seasoning.

3. Drain any excess water from the paste ingredients and knead the cracked wheat until it forms a firm paste, using a food processor if possible.

4. Either mould the paste into cigar shapes as explained above and fill with the meat mixture

or/ Oil the bottom of a deep baking dish and spread over half the paste. Spoon over the meat and top with the remaining paste. Dribble over about 2 tablespoons olive oil to moisten the surface of the pourgouri paste.

5. To cook the koupes: fry in hot oil until crisp and golden brown.
   To cook the tray: bake in a moderate oven for 30-40 minutes.

6. Serve the Koupes or Tray Kibbeh with a very good squeeze of lemon juice.

ΣΧΟΛΙΚΑ ΕΙΔΗ
ΦΕΙΔΙΑΣ ΠΑΝΑΓΙΩΤΟΥ

KENT
SENIOR SERVICE
SENIOR SERVICE

• Marrow Flower Fritters with Tomato Sauce •

Boxes of bright yellow marrow flowers catch the eye of every passerby in the market. But how many visitors must wonder what the Cypriots do with them? Well of course they eat them! The Cypriots eat almost everything that grows and these delicate yellow trumpets with their powdery pin head stigma are cooked in a number of ways. Stuffed marrow flowers are a favourite, using a rice and vegetable mixture with a little minced meat and some fresh herbs, or the flowers are dipped in batter and served crisply fried.

If you can't find any marrow flowers then use the actual marrow or courgettes, grated straight into the batter. It makes a delicate dish and the tomato sauce helps to bring out the flavour.

Serve the fritters on their own as a first course or as part of a larger meal.

• Serves 4 •

Ingredients

For the fritters

a handful of fresh marrow flowers/or

1lb (450g) marrow peeled and deseeded

1 egg

salt and pepper

3 tablespoons flour

oil for frying

For the Sauce

1½lb (750g) ripe tomatoes, roughly chopped

2 cloves garlic, chopped

sprig of rosemary, thyme or fresh basil

salt and pepper

a pinch of sugar

1. First make up the tomato sauce: Cook the tomatoes, garlic and herbs together over a low heat until most of the liquid has evaporated. Press through a fine sieve. Add salt, pepper and sugar. Re-heat when ready to serve.

2. For the fritters: Make a batter with the egg, salt and pepper and 3 tablespoons of flour.

Either drop the flowers into this batter until they are well coated or grate the marrow straight into it.

3. Heat the oil and fry the battered flowers or desertspoonfuls of the grated marrow mixture for about two minutes.

4. Serve at once with the warm tomato sauce.

• Psarosoupa — Fish Soup •

Andreas' taverna is nothing more than a wooden shack with no running water and only an old generator for electricity, but it sits on the rocks overlooking pretty Melanda bay. The area is completely unspoilt and for this reason we creep off to the peace and quiet that Andreas and his wife offer during the tourist season in Cyprus.

I well remember one evening in high summer when we arrived early to enjoy the sun before it set. Although nothing appeared to be in the least prepared for the advancing evening eaters, Andreas greeted us with the good news that fish soup was on the menu, and he himself had caught the fish and was making the soup.

Well, we quelled our appetites with some dips and then a few kebabs with some salad, followed by fresh fruit. It was just as we called for the bill that Andreas finally appeared, beaming from ear to ear, with a large bowl of freshly made fish soup. It tasted superb even in our full stomachs!

• Serves 4-6 •

Ingredients

2 tablespoons sunflower or olive oil

1 large onion, sliced

1 clove garlic, crushed

3 large juicy tomatoes or / 2 tablespoons concentrated tomato puree

3lb (1½ k) assorted small fish or heads, tails and bones!

1 glass/200ml dry white wine

2 tablespoons chopped parsley

small piece lemon peel

salt and pepper

1. Heat the oil in a large saucepan and gently fry the onion and garlic till soft but not brown.

2. Add the grated fresh tomatoes or tomato puree.

3. Add the cleaned fish, wine, parsley, lemon peel and seasoning.

4. Add enough water to cover all the ingredients and bring to the boil. Cover the pan and simmer for 30 minutes.

5. Strain the soup and reheat.

6. Serve with chunks of fresh bread.

• Kidonobasto — Quince Paste•

Quinces or **kidonia** hold a place of importance on the island of Cyprus for the quince was the golden apple that Paris awarded to Aphrodite, and it became her fruit; the fruit of love, marriage and fertility.

In spring the scent of the flowering quince trees is inspirational, but it is not until the autumn that the large ugly looking fruits appeared in the market. Stewed or combined with apples the scent again emerges and the Cypriots use their kidonia in a variety of ways.

Quince paste is made in many mediterranean countries and makes an exceptionally nice sweetmeat.

Ingredients

4lb (2kg) quinces
1 glass/ ½ pint water
sugar to taste
juice of 1 lemon

1. Wash and cut up the quinces, having first rubbed off grey fluff from the skin.

2. Put them into a heavy pan with the water. Bring to the boil and simmer gently until the fruit is tender. Beat with a wooden spoon to break up the quinces and when they are very soft, press through a wire sieve.

3. Weigh the sieved puree and put it back into the rinsed out pan with an equal weight of sugar. Stir over low heat until the sugar has dissolved then add the lemon juice. Raise the heat and boil until the mixture thickens and candies, leaving the sides of the pan and turning dark red. Stir all the time but take care that the boiling puree doesn't spit and burn you.

4. When the paste is really thick pour it into a shallow tin lined with greaseproof or oiled paper and spread it out with a spatula.

Put the tray in a warm place and leave for a couple of days to dry.

Finally cut the quince paste into squares and either serve it as it is or dust lightly with caster or icing sugar.

• Spanakopitta—Spinach in Filo Pastry •

Fyllo in Greek means a leaf and this is also the name of the wafer thin Greek pastry that is used so successfully in the preparation of Middle Eastern pastries.

Filo is now available in Greek shops, delicatessens and most large supermarkets. If you use it from frozen thaw gently in the fridge and once the packet is opened keep the pastry leaves covered with a damp cloth to prevent them drying out.

Filo pastry is so simple to cook with, if you have any sheets left over experiment with them by adding your own fillings, sweet or savoury and wrapping them into tiny surprise bundles. Brush with melted butter and bake in a moderate oven until golden brown.

• Makes over 6 •

Ingredients

2lbs (1 kilo) fresh spinach, washed and chopped
3-4 tablespoons olive oil
1 bunch spring onions, finely chopped
salt and freshly ground black pepper
2 tablespoons chopped parsley
½ teaspoon grated nutmeg
4oz (100g) feta cheese (or cheddar), crumbled
2-3 eggs, slightly beaten
8-10 sheets filo pastry
4oz (100g) butter

I find that aluminium gives spinach a definite metallic flavour so avoid cooking in it if you can.

1. Heat the oil and fry the spring onions gently without browning for a few minutes. Add the drained spinach and toss until it begins to wilt. Cover and cook gently for 5 minutes.

2. Allow the spinach to cool a little before adding salt, pepper, parsley, nutmet, cheese and the eggs.

3. Melt the butter and spread some over the base of a large, deep, square or round baking tin or oven dish.

4. Fit four or five sheets of filo pastry in the bottom, brushing between each layer with melted butter.

5. Spoon the spinach filling over the filo sheets and cover with the remaining filo, separated by melted butter as before.

6. Tuck the sides under neatly and brush butter over the top of the pie.

7. Bake your spanakopitta in a medium oven Gas 4, 350°F , 180°C for about 40 minutes then increase the heat for another 5 minutes to crisp the top.

Serve hot, warm or cold.

• Tabbouleh — Cracked Wheat Salad•

Tabbouleh must be the simplest and quickest grain salad to rustle up in a jiffy.

It is an Arab salad, eaten extensively throughout the Middle East and is deliciously refreshing. Made from pourgouri or cracked wheat, the pre-cooked grains only need to be soaked for 15 minutes in cold water before they are ready to toss with the remaining ingredients and serve.

• Serves 4-6 •

Ingredients

100g (4oz) pourgouri
juice of 2 lemons
salt and pepper
5 tablespoons olive oil
1 very large bunch of parsley, finely chopped
6 spring onions or 1 small onion, finely chopped
fresh mint, as much as you like, chopped
3 tomatoes, diced
large crisp lettuce leaves to line the salad bowl

1. Soak the pourgouri in cold water for 15 minutes then strain in a sieve and press out the surplus water.

2. Mix with lemon juice, salt and pepper and leave for another 15 minutes to swell.

3. Stir in the oil, herbs and onion.

4. Line a salad bowl with the lettuce leaves, spoon in the Tabbouleh and arrange the chopped tomato on top for decoration.

• Arnaki Me Fasolakia Yachni — Lamb and French Bean Casserole •

In Cyprus yachni denotes that the dish is prepared and cooked with tomatoes. A very common way of cooking in Cyprus due, no doubt, to the fantastic crop of tomatoes!

Vegetables are quite often cooked 'yachni' without meat, but my favourite is this combination of lamb and green beans.

On one of those very rare wet and windy days in Cyprus we found ourselves on a remote mountain road in the Pitzillia region of Cyprus.

Doors were tightly shut against the weather and we could find no sign of the usual hospitality that characterises the Cypriots.

Finally we searched out the pale blue door in the centre of Agros and knew that our worries were over. Pots, pans and dishes full of the most enticing smells were piled haphazardly on a small range and we settled immediately into the cosy atmosphere. The owner/cook/waiter reeled off the menu from memory and was a little surprised when we enthusiastically ordered one of everything! He agreed to bring small portions and we stayed a long time . . . well, why not, the sun was bound to come out later!

The Syrians also have a stew called a Yakhnie which they serve, no doubt, with pourgouri or burghul like the Cypriots. Potatoes, though, are a major crop on the island and Cypriots generally like to eat roast potatoes with their casseroles.

• Serves 4-6 •

Ingredients

2lbs (1 kilo) lean lamb diced into 4cm cubes

4 tablespoons cooking oil

1 large onion, sliced

2lbs (1 kilo) cooking tomatoes, skinned and chopped

1 good tablespoon tomato puree

1 teaspoon rigani, marjoram or oregano

8oz (225g) french or runner beans, trimmed and cut in half

salt and black pepper

potatoes, peeled (optional)

1. Heat the oil in a heavy based casserole. Fry the meat, a few cubes at a time, adding more oil if necessary. Remove and keep warm.

2. Fry the onion gently for five minutes. Add the tomatoes and stir well to break up. Season well and add the puree and herbs. Replace the meat into the casserole.

3. Add water if necessary to ensure that the meat is covered by the tomatoes.

4. Cover and cook gently on top of the cooker or in a slow oven Gas 2, 300°F, 150°C for about an hour or until the lamb is tender.

5. Add the beans and potatoes, add a little more water if necessary. Continue to cook till the vegetables are done, then remove the lid and let the juices boil a little to thicken the sauce if necessary.

• Yemista — Stuffed Vegetables •

Yemista comes from the Greek verb **yiemizo** to fill, and the Cypriot style of stuffed vegetables certainly bears more resemblance to the Greek recipe than any other neighbour in the Levant.

Stuffed vegetables are prepared all over the Mediterranean, and have been since the Ottoman Empire, if not before.

Eyecatching for visitors, these trays of mixed vegetables laden with fillings are on the taverna menus during the autumn.

Yogurt, dried fruit and nuts are common ingredients in Greek 'dolmas' or stuffed vegetables, whilst in Armenia you may find cracked wheat. In Egypt and Syria spices play an important part and even pulses find their way into yemistas!

Meat is not a vital ingredient in Cypriot yemista, its inclusion is rather up to the individual. Dried fruit, such as raisins or currants and even nuts are rarely used, since Cypriots seldom mix sweet and savoury flavours in a dish.

Parsley, rice, oil and a little onion form the basic filling which is stuffed into peppers, aubergines, onions, tomatoes, courgettes, and best of all, large yellow courgette flowers.

Ingredients

2lbs (1kg) fresh, crisp unblemished vegetables
2 tablespoons olive oil
2 onions, finely chopped
4oz (100g) long grain white rice
4oz (100g) minced meat (optional)
1 tablespoon chopped fresh mint
2 tablespoons chopped parsley
juice of a lemon
½ teaspoon ground cinnamon
salt and pepper
1 tablespoon olive oil
1 tablespoon tomato puree diluted with ½ glass/100ml water

1. Prepare the vegetables.

Peppers, cut the top off and keep them to put back on later. Discard the seeds.

Aubergines, cut the top off and keep them. Scoop out the middle and add it to the filling.

Courgettes, cut lengthways, scoop out the middle and add to the filling.

Tomatoes, cut off the tops, keep them. Scoop out the filling, strain the pips and add the pulp to the filling. Sprinkle some sugar into the hollow tomatoes.

Large onions, cut off both ends and push the middle out. Chop and add it to the filling instead of the onion in the recipe.

2. Fry the onion in the oil until it begins to colour. Stir in the rice and meat if you are using it. Stir and cook until the rice turns transparent and the meat looses its redness. Add the herbs and seasoning.

3. Spoon the filling into the prepared vegetables, replace their lids.

4. Arrange them snugly in a casserole dish. Wedge some slices of potato between the vegetables if necessary to keep them upright in the dish.

5. Mix the tomato puree with the water and pour this over the vegetables together with the tablespoonful of olive oil.

6. Bake in a moderate oven Gas No. 5, 375°F, 190°C for about an hour. Check every 15 minutes to baste the vegetables adding more stock or tomato paste and water if necessary.

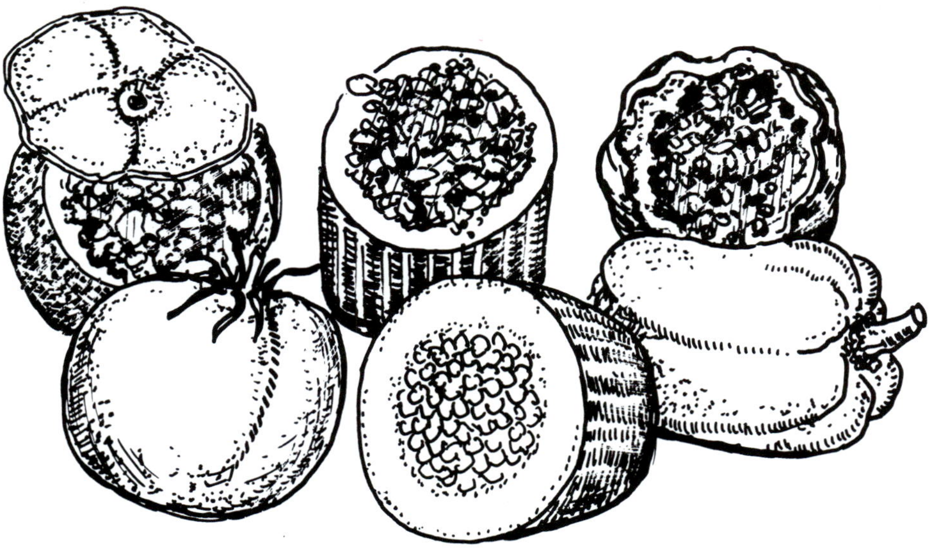

Winter

When it rains in Cyprus, it really rains. The sky blackens, thunder and lightning roll and the roads turn into canals of rushing water. So sudden are these storms that one feels a sense of miraculous survival once they have passed.

Winter brings what bad weather there is in Cyprus. But even then hardly a day passes without the sight of blue sky.

The courtyard is finally deserted by Cypriot families who reluctantly bring the chairs, tables and sometimes the beds into the house.

These winter months are a time to replenish stocks. Preserves like glyko, fruit soaked in heavy syrup, are made now and the autumn crops of nuts and olive stored away safely.

Fish, more plentiful during the winter months is smoked, salted or pickled. Prior to Christmas the Greek Orthodox church decree a fast for forty days and this frugal diet of no meat or dairy produce gives the body a health cure.

Preparations for Christmas start with the slaughter of the pig so that the meat can be prepared and preserved in a variety of ways.

Enticing smells waft out of Cypriot kitchens as Christmas baking appears. Everything is baked in enormous quantities to be shared throughout the family. And the families gather to celebrate Christmas and enjoy many of the religious and superstitious customs together. Christmas in Cyprus is a time for giving and presents of traditional biscuits like melomakarona are handed from house to house.

But once Christmas and the New Year are over it is back to work with a vengeance in Cyprus. Epiphany brings with it the hope for fruitful crops and prosperity for the forthcoming year.

Already the citrus crop is ripe for harvesting and lorries carry their loads of oranges and grapefruit to the fruit pressing plants.

Artichokes, avocados, cauliflowers and cabbages fill the market place. While the farmers sew new crops and pruning begins on the vines the air is full of optimism for the people of Cyprus believe, as in the words of a Greek proverb

"Next year's wine is the sweetest".

CHRISTMAS IN CYPRUS

Christmas in Cyprus is a simple family celebration. It comes second in importance to Easter in the Greek Orthodox Calendar, but nevertheless, commercialism is quick to catch on, and the shops overflow with gifts. Many Cypriots still fast for 40 days before Christmas, eating no meat or dairy products but due to the recent olive harvest, no-one lacks for olive oil!

During Advent all diligent housewives will clean their houses from top to bottom before heading for the shops to buy a new set of clothes for Christmas.

Many of the widows simply replace their black clothes with the same and the men in the villages may perhaps have a new pair of the baggy black trousers or vraka made. Here is a Cypriot poem about them . . .

"With forty pics of material
One makes one vraka
which sweeps the earth,
poor old vraka
which sounds like triki-traka.

Pork is generally the meat of the Christmas feast. The pig, first a damned and later a holy animal, was considered a symbol of fertility, mainly due to its black earthy colour. Goddesses of fertility such as Aphrodite, Demeter, and her daughter Persephone, all had the pig as their symbol.

The butchering of the pig is a very old tradition dating back to when the ancient Greeks sacrificed pigs at the feast of Skirophoria. It is a very social occasion and one to be celebrated by the whole village community.

In rural areas every family used to raise a pig throughout the year, in order to fatten it up for the Christmas feast.

The pig was first butchered by the man of the house, and the meat was then sprinkled with salt and coriander, the latter being a magic herb which keeps away evil.

If the pig didn't become as plump as desired, it was said to be because the animal had dreamt about its coming fate on the night of St. Spiridon's day. The dream worried the pig and caused it to lose its appetite!

From the pig the villagers make **loukanika,** the Cypriot sausages which are smoked over sticks just before Christmas. The leg of pork is cured in wine then hung in the chimney to smoke, in time maturing to become **hiromeri. Lounza,** the smoked loin of pork is also a traditional Christmas food. The fat of the pig is rendered down and then made into **titsiripittes** or pasties, and the pigs head and trotters are turned into **zalatina** or brawn. Small pieces of meat soaked in wine and conserved in lard are called **koumnista.**

Just a few weeks before Christmas, baking gets under way. Christmas cakes in Cyprus bear a distinct similarity to the British Christmas cake and it is reasonable to see the link since the British have dwelt on the island for a hundred years or so. But there is a subtle difference in the texture and substance of the Cypriot cake and I like it the better of the two. Much of the dried fruit that we use is exchanged for glyko (fruit steeped in syrup) and there are many more eggs and nuts used in Cyprus. No wonder, since they are the more common ingredients on the island.

Powdery icing sugar covered **kourabiedes** or shortbread biscuits are baked and **melomakarona,** spicy buns drenched in honey syrup and in most households a special round bread with a candle in the middle is prepared called a **Christocouloura.**

An essential part of Christmas in Cyprus are the mythical creatures called ***kalikanzari.*** Cypriot folklaw tells us that these naughty little goblins may appear at any time during the twelve days of Christmas to disturb the peace, or even pinch you, and it is wise to throw some cakes up on to the roof to keep them happy!

Father Christmas doesn't visit Cyprus, instead St. Basil brings a sack of toys for the children. He arrives on New Year's Eve in time to celebrate the New Year which is also known as St. Basil's Day.

Christians believe that St. Basil brings new year's gifts of prosperity for the houses and fruitfulness for the soil and he also may bring love and happiness to the unmarried fraternity.

To test this superstition green olive branches are collected and burnt over an open fire, and if they crack and jump, then the lovesick youngster is reassured of his/her's partners attention.

Here is the poem attached to this custom

Saint Basil, King of January and Knight
let me go down into the desert, let me
go down into Hell; show and reveal
if he or she loves me

New Year's morning and the **vasilopitta** or St. Basil's cake is cut. The first slice is given to the church, the second to the poor, the third is cut for the house and the rest of the cake is divided between the members of the family, starting with the most senior. Hidden in its midst of this large cake is a coin and whoever finds it is guaranteed luck for the coming year.

The story behind St. Basil goes . . .
'When Caesarea was being attacked by the Cappadocians St Basil appealed to his people to help in the form of giving something of value. By a miracle the Cappadonians gave up their attack and St Basil, finding himself surrounded by valuables, baked some loaves in which he hid the precious objects'.

Everyone is happy on New Year's Day because Cypriots believe that they should behave in a way they wish to follow for the following year. The children find it the ideal day to call on relatives who give generously. On the sixth of January, the twelfth and last day of

Christmas, Cypriots celebrate *Ta Fota* — the Baptism of Christ or Epiphany.

The blessing or the water is celebrated throughout the island and in most coastal towns a very special ceremony takes place.

After a church service a band strikes up to lead the procession to the sea. The archbishop or bishop throws his cross into the water. At the same time 2 white doves are released to symbolize the Holy Ghost. Brave young men dive for the cross and the one who collects it is blessed for the year.

In most areas of Cyprus people take fruit, vegetables or grain to be dipped in the holy water to baptise them . . . thus bringing a good harvest and a renewal of life throughout the land.

BREAD AND BAKING

"A fool throws a stone into the sea and a hundred wise men cannot pull it out"

Greek proverb.

As a visitor to Cyprus you may well be confused by the enormous variety of bread for sale. Not so long ago the decision would have been made for you — there was only one type of loaf on offer!

But baking in Cyprus is changing. It must adjust to the demands of the many different nationalities that now live on the island. Methods of baking are changing too.

Let's start by visiting a village bakery.

Here you will see traditional bread, baked in a solid fuel oven.

A basic round disc of bread with a good unbroken crust, weighing about a kilo. This is made from blends of flour, incorporating duram wheat which gives it the characteristic yellow-white colour. Apart from yeast, water and salt nothing else is added to the flour. Notice the raised lid which is made by the baker cutting the soft dough with a sharp knife in a circle around the top outer rim. The texture of this loaf is close and it cuts easily. This bread, due to the government subsidies is sold for just 15 cents a loaf. It will be eaten by most of the villagers with most meals.

For breakfast a popular bread also sold in village bakeries is the koulouri loaf. It resembles a row of finger rolls which are stuck together and the top is beautifully brown and covered with poppy and sesame seeds. The top grade flour only is used for koulouri and it costs 25c for a loaf weighing less than a kilo. The inside of the loaf is soft, white and puffy. It is best eaten fresh when you really taste the extra flavours of a little cinnamon and some ground mastica.

Now let's move on to a modern commercial bakery.

The main difference will be in the large variety of breads for sale and the more modern equipment used to produce them. Steam ovens are by far the most popular now. They require little time to heat, and produce, on the whole, a more moist and good looking bread. That is not to say that the bread will last very long, for it will not, compared to traditional village bakery bread. Of course the basic round loaf is for sale at 15 cents, but for another 10 cents there are a whole new selection to choose from. These loaves appear in the same shape but contain a variety of blends and qualities of flour. You can choose between a sesame seed coated loaf to a brown one that has a high proportion of bran added. There will be a wheatbread made with the top grade flour and this loaf is lighter in texture and better flavoured than the basic loaf.

Koulouri is always on sale with its aromatic light textured middle and a variety of seeds on top for decoration. But take a look at the other small cakes and pies such as **halumopittes** cheese pies, **eliopittes** olive bread or pies, **kolokopittes** pumpkin pies, and the most popular of all, the tahinopittes made from sweet sesame seed paste.

Biscuits, too, in all shapes and sizes as well as the pastries. Rows and rows of **baklava, kateyfi** and **pishides** all dripping with syrup and so good to eat.

But when it comes to baking should you not also sample the flavours of home cooking. Choose a friend who is not only a Cypriot but also a good cook, perhaps the two are synonymous!

Home baking will always have advantages over the commercial bakeries. Not for bread perhaps when the selection, price and convenience of traditional bread outweighs the time and effort of the home cook. But take pastries, what can be more satisfying than to cook in the familiarity of your own kitchen, in your own time and adding those extra flavours that make such a difference.

Try baking **baklava** and **kateyfi;** they are not complicated to prepare, especially if you buy the ready made filo pastry. How different they taste though, when soaked in a little homemade syrup of honey, lemon juice and rose water rather than the bakery sugar syrup. Chop the nuts you prefer, add a little grated lemon rind or cinnamon and personalise your pastries. Many pastries found in Cyprus are deep fried, such as **daktyla** and **loukmades.** Having prepared the pastry and filling, satisfy yourself that the pastries are cooked in good quality clean oil and then drained immediately allowing excess fat to drain off. **Bourekia,** little pastry turnovers which can have a savoury or sweet filling also benefit from the home touch.

Different foods and flavours give the visitor an insight into a foreign place. So, while in Cyprus, taste all manner of local specialities that come your way. Nibble a pastry while you shop in the market, sample a slice of something with your next coffee, and don't turn anything down offered when visiting a traditional village festival.

If you visit the mountain villages of Omodos or Vasa you may find one of the more unusual breads baked on the island. It is called **arkadena** and is a sour-dough bread made from a fermentation of chick peas. It tastes best fresh but you are more likely to find it dry and crisp.

Of all the baking in Cyprus there is one speciality that outshines all others, this is the **Flaouna.** Prepared by every woman on the island, whether housewife, professional baker, grandmother or modern office girl . . . these are the Easter speciality for the Cypriots. Ingredients vary depending on which region the recipe originated but usually include a little mint, sometimes baked and ground hemp seed, more often than not a handful of raisins and the mastic gum flavouring too.

One of the more unusual flavouring which you find in Flaounas as well as other Cypriot baking is mahlabe. This is the kernel from the cherry stone, which, when crushed gives a strong, slightly bitter cherry or almond flavour.

We all know that pastries are a delight to the eye and a threat to the waistline, but if you, like me, are a pastry freak, then let's revel in the unusual flavours of this Levantine corner of the Mediterranean and nibble a pastry or two too many.

CYPRUS CHEESES

"If God had not made brown honey men would think figs much sweeter than they do"

(Xenophanes)

A glass of wine and a chunk of cheese: who needs more?

In Cyprus you can sample the very best of both, for wine and cheese have been here almost as long as civilization itself.

It seems likely that the recipe for cheese was first stumbled upon in the Middle East, because traces of cheese are said to have been found in the tomb of the dynastic Pharaoh Horus. Almost five thousand years ago the Sumerians made a magnificent bas-relief, aptly known as the Dairy Frieze which demonstrates the complete cheesemaking process from milking the animals to curdling the milk. The same principles apply today.

There is a legend that tells of how some Arab herdsmen took a supply of milk on a journey in a pouch made from a sheep's stomach. On opening the pouch they found not milk but curds, caused by the heat, the jolting camel ride, and the rennet in the sheep's stomach.

Such a simple food has always been the staple of the peasant and yet a luxury to the wealthy. In ancient Greece, cheese was chosen as part of the controlled diet of athletes, and when Alexander the Great defeated Darius at Damascus in 331BC the vanquished Persian king fled leaving behind his 500 cooks, 13 of whom were experts at processing milk to make cheeses for his table. In Imperial Rome there were at least 13 different styles being made and cheese was imported from as far away as Britain and the Pyrenees.

Cyprus still has a dependence on dairy farming, were animal husbandry comes as second nature to the rural communities. Watch the shepherds and goat herdsmen moving their flocks to find the best forage. Sheep, goats, as well as cows, provide milk for cheesemaking and there are a variety of cheeses available. The best-known and most consumed cheese in Cyprus today is **halloumi,** a white, often mint-flavoured cheese which is part of the daily diet of every Cypriot family. **Anari** and **kefalotiri** are popular too as well as **feta,** the salty Greek cheese.

Those cheeses made in the early summer are the best to sample for they are made from the milk of animals which have grazed on lush spring vegetation. Goats' milk is fairly thin but makes a strongly flavoured cheese, while ewes milk is altogether thicker and richer. Cows' milk mixes well with both these and more often than not a combination of milks is used in Cypriot cheeses. Of course the flavour of the cheeses varies according to local vegetation and individual methods of making, as well as the freshness of the milk and the temperature of the air.

Today in Cyprus, much of the cheese you find in the grocers and supermarkets is factory made. Milk from all the rural areas is collected in large tankers and on arrival at the factory it is pasteurised. This seems extremely wise since the temperatures soar in the summer months.

The cheese is vacuum packed which keeps it fresh for longer.

Perhaps you prefer a more individual homemade cheese though and for these you must look at the market stalls.

Homemade cheese is still made in all the rural villages of Cyprus just as it was at the turn of the century.

Cheese-making on a small scale is the perfect part-time job for busy village women and the extra income it brings in is always a welcome addition to the meagre budget of a rural family.

Two or three times a week, as soon as enough fresh goats or ewe's milk has accumulated, it is set to boil in an enormous coppered cauldron or hartchi.

Halloumi and **feta** cheeses are the easiest to make. They can be prepared from any combination of milk and the basic equipment is always to hand. Usually about 50 kilos of milk are used at one time. It is first heated and then the powdered rennet added to make it curdle. The curds, once set, are cut and scooped out of the whey. Feta is left to drain naturally in a large square block which is then cut into smaller blocks and salted before being immersed in brine to mature. Halloumi has slightly more rennet added; the curds are pressed to express the whey and it is then cooked again. This differing process gives it the characteristic firm, almost rubbery texture, and a long life when it is preserved in brine.

But that's not all, there is another cheese yet to be made out of the same milk. This is a low fat, full protein soft cheese called **anari** similar to Italian ricotta. The whey that drains out of the milk when the curds set for the halloumi and feta is reheated and the crumbly soft white cheese rises to the surface. It is skimmed off and left to drain in attractive reed baskets called **dalari.**

Anari can be eaten fresh, in fact the fresher the better. The Cypriots simply spread it on fresh bread. It makes a very good cheesecake but I like anari best in bourekia where it is mixed with honey and spice and wrapped in filo pastry.

Salted anari will last a little longer and can be eaten alone or as part of a mezé.

Anari can also be left to dry to a hard compact full flavoured cheese. This is the Cypriot alternative to parmesan and grates well.

Feta, of course, graces every **salata khoriatiki** or village salad. Its salty crumbly taste blends perfectly with acid tomatoes, crunchy cumcumber, freshly chopped herbs and onions. Olive oil and lemon juice mixed, in a proportion of 3 to 1 make the perfect dressing. Feta cooks well too. Combined with fresh spinach and beaten egg it adds a salty tang to **spanakopitta,** the filo pastry pie of spinach.

As for halloumi, the king of Cyprus cheeses, just eat it as it is. But if your barbecue is alight, then why not grill some slices gently over the glowing charcoal. Softening from the warmth, but slightly crisp and brown at the edges, grilled halloumi has a mellow flavour of its own, which can only be enhanced by, perhaps, a sprinkling of freshly chopped mint and a squeeze of fresh lemon.

The best way to get to know 'foreign' cheese is to taste it and I shall leave you with a basic vocabulary of words that you will find useful when buying cheese in Cyprus.

KATSIKA — goat
AGELADA — cow
PROVATINA — ewe
ELAFRO — mild
FRESCO — fresh
MALAKO — soft
PALIO — mature
PIKANTIKO — sharp
SKLIRO — hard
TROHALO — curd
OROS — whey

PSARI — FISH

Fishing runs in the blood of most Cypriots. Any day of the year, and most nights too, finds a bunch of local fishermen in their small boats, throwing out their nets not far from the shore.

These small-time fishermen either sell their catch to a chain of taverna owners or else they fish by night and run their own tavernas by day.

I remember how one Sunday as we lunched in the winter sunshine at Pissouri we were offered cuttlefish by the proprietor. Were they fresh, we asked "Of course, said Pepi, I caught them myself this morning, here in the bay".

On the whole fish is expensive in Cyprus because there just isn't much of it in the sea at this far Eastern end of the Mediterranean. Apart from the local fishermen much of the fish we find in the market is caught by trawlers who drag their nets along the sea floor. They catch anything and everything, and in order to preserve these fish stocks they are restricted to trawling only over the winter months.

Further off shore the sea bed is incredibly deep and the Cypriot fishermen have been encouraged to distant water trawl, even as far away as the Egyptian coast. The department of Fisheries within the

Ministry of Agriculture and Natural Resources offer incentives to these fishermen in the hope that the younger fish near the Cyprus coast will have a chance to mature.

It's a fine sight to watch the catch coming home. Sitting by the harbour at the fishing port of Latchi on the western coast of the island one day in late June we saw five massive swordfish brought ashore. Each carried majestically up the jetty on the shoulders of a proud fisherman, the swords pointing forwards and anything up to two and a half feet in length.

Pollution in the sea around the coast of Cyprus is also a problem for fishing, for this far eastern corner of the Mediterranean has little chance of a flush system. But the Suez canal has brought a small influx of new water and a few interesting and unusual species of fish over the past few decades.

Sadly the sword fish and natural sponges have both suffered from disease as have the green turtles but not now since they were made a protected species in Cyprus and encourage to breed on the Akamas peninsula to the north east of Paphos, in Lara's bay.

Fish farms are springing up all around the coast, especially in the Paphos, Akrotiri and Larnaca areas. Fish culture both in sea water and fresh is encouraged by the government and fish such as trout, sea bass, sea bream and white bream are reared in on-shore sea water tanks.

The many reservoirs constructed recently, which have so successfully extinguished the 'water worry' for islanders during the summer months are now being tested for fresh water fish culture. Trout, atlantic salmon, eels, bass, tench, carp, perch, silver bream and grey mullet are all being farmed in these dams.

So with all this chat about catching fish, let's take a look at the cooking.

How do Cypriots like to eat fish?

For a large gathering nothing would please a Cypriot family more than a whole large fish baked in the oven with a selection of vegetables.

Grilled fish, large or small are also popular, served with salad. For some of the smaller fish or those with less oil in their flesh, frying is the best answer.

Octopus, cuttle fish and squid have always been favourites in Cyprus, and compared to the high cost of most fish bought on the island, they are a bargain.

What fish can you, as a visitor, expect to find in the restaurants and tavernas?

The answer is — whatever came in on the boat today! Although frozen imported fish is now available at most supermarkets, it is regarded with great suspicion; the Cypriots like their food fresh.

So let's stick to the fresh variety, and take a look at the market stalls. No doubt there will be glistening silvery mounds of ***marida,*** brown picarel. They are something like an anchovy or a small sardine. Buy them small, dip in a light batter and fry like whitebait. They can be rather bony and their flavour is greatly improved with fresh lemon juice. Marida cost very little.

Pretty ***barbourni*** or red mullet will catch your eye, no doubt. A good fish to grill or fry. Serve with a dribble of good quality olive oil, a squeeze of lemon and a handful of freshly chopped parsley. In Cyprus barbouni are fished very small, often only about 10 cms, and can make quite a bony mouthful. How I wish these pretty little fish were left in the sea to grow a bit!

Grey mullet or ***cephalos*** are a delicious fish to grill but harder to find than the red mullet.

The ***synagrida*** or dentex is popular here, usually grilled if small, or baked if large. It is silver sided but has a darker, almost blue back.

Belonging to the same family are the breams. ***Sparos, sargos, mourmoura*** and ***melana*** are all varieties of bream found off the coast of Cyprus, perhaps the best known are ***lithrini*** red bream or pandora, and king of all breams ***fangri.***

These breams all have firm flesh and will grill well as long as they are kept moist with oil during the cooking. Baked as in the Psari Plaki recipe or Psari Sto Fourno, these breams make a succulent and complete dish.

Palamida or atlantic little tuna is a member of the thunnidae family. Due to their oily flesh the Cypriots regard these as 'heavy' fish and they are best baked in the oven with onions and tomatoes. Alternatively, these small tuna can be poached in a court bouillon and served with egg and lemon sauce (avgolemoni).

The bass family known as ***vlachos*** and ***sphyrida*** are common fish on the market fish stands. They are from the sea bass family and taste better fried rather than grilled due to their lack of natural oil. Again the larger specimens would be better baked with vegetables.

Volonida, zarganes or garfish are delicious and worth buying on sight. They are a dark metal colour and very slim with a long pointed nose. ***Gofari*** or bluefish are found in abundance near the Turkish coast and sometimes they swim south! One of the most expensive fish to buy is the ***xiphias*** or sword fish. This is highly rated by the Cypriots and swordfish steaks are favourite taverna fare. Check that your xiphias is fresh though, for the sword fish are extremely large and during the heat of summer, keeping a whole fish fresh is not easy.

The cephalopods, octopus ***octapodhi,*** squid ***kalamari,*** and cuttlefish ***sepia*** or ***soupies*** are plentiful and cheap all the year round.

The excitement on the quay as an octopus is brought ashore is magnetic. Crowds gather and quite often the poor beast gets beaten there and then. Not that beating an octopus is so unusual. In fact no octopus is worth cooking until it has been extremely well beaten to soften the flesh. A modern method of battering octopus is to spin it hard in an old washing machine! Find a fishmonger or fisherman who you trust and ask them to beat and clean your fish, as though it were destined for their own table!

Octopus hanging to dry in the sun is a common sight. Once dry they keep indefinitely, and just need a good soaking to transform them into a tasty dish.

A good way with octopus is to stew it first in its own juices and then cook gently with wine and onions. Fried or grilled octopus with an oil, lemon and parsley dressing is delicious in the summer heat, and in tavernas it often appears as part of a mezé.

Both squid and cuttlefish are worth trying if you haven't cooked them before. They are nourishing, inexpensive, delicious and really not difficult to prepare. All the recipes give full preparation instructions.

Two fish that have arrived in coastal waters of Cyprus since the opening of the Suez canal are *siganos* or the rabbit fish and *rossos* or red soldier fish.

The last fish worth mentioning is ***bakaliaros.*** Salted cod, a traditional Lenten ingredient, but also frequently eaten during the winter. Salt cod should be soaked overnight to remove the excessive salty flavour. I like it best, poached and served cold with *skordalia,* or garlic sauce.

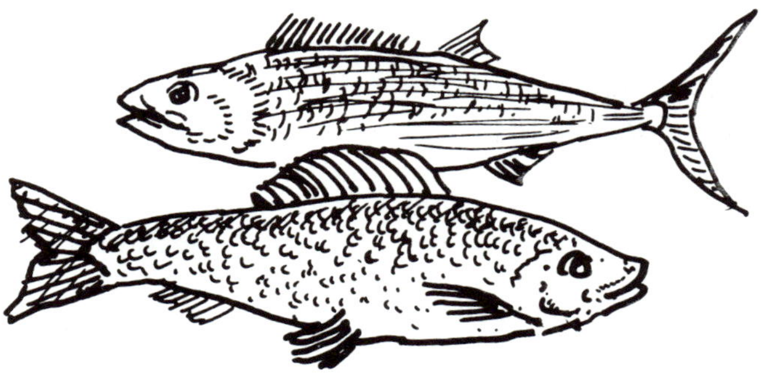

• Sikoti Afelia — Liver with Wine Sauce •

Offal is often cooked in Cypriot homes but not so often offered in restaurants and tavernas. The Cypriots cook liver well, either lightly fried, grilled or cooked with onions and wine as in this recipe for liver afelia.

I remember eating liver at the rustic Flamingo taverna which sits at the edge of the salt lake on the outskirts of Larnaca.

Larnaca is named after Lazarus, friend of Christ, who fled to Cyprus from the persecution of the Jews. There is a legend which tells how Lazarus once found himself thirsty in the region of the salt lake. It was at that time a thriving vineyard owned by an old woman. She refused to allow Lazarus a bunch of grapes to quench his thirst, saying that the place produced nothing but salt. As the Saint turned to leave he replied to her "Good woman, may your vineyard product nothing but salt". On the spot the vineyard withered and in its place appeared the present salt lake.

• Serves 4-6 •

Ingredients

1lb (450g) lamb's liver

5 tablespoons olive oil

1 medium onion, finely sliced

4 tablespoons red wine

2 tablespoons red wine vinegar

1 teaspoon coriander seeds, crushed roughly

½ teaspoon ground cinnamon

juice of ½ lemon

salt and freshly ground black pepper

1. Slice the liver in thick, mouthful sized portions.

2. Heat the oil in a large frying pan and brown the liver over a brisk heat.

3. Add the onion, lower the heat a little and saute the onion and liver together for 2-3 more minutes.

4. As the liver juices begin to run, add all the other ingredients, apart from the lemon juice. Cover the pan and simmer for 20 minutes or until most of the moisture has evaporated and a smooth sauce remains.

5. Sprinkle the lemon juice all over and serve at once with saute or jacket potatoes and a salad.

• Avocado Dip •

Avocados are a recent arrival in Cyprus. Famous for their cultivation in Israel, not surprisingly, Cyprus too has the right growing conditions for this vegetable.

The Cypriots are reserved about their food though, and it takes time for a new ingredient to become fully integrated into the diet. At a pound for a kilo they are definitely a good buy and this dip is one of the best ways to serve them.

Don't forget to collect some pitta bread too when you go shopping!

• Serves 4 •

Ingredients

2 ripe avocado pears

2 cloves garlic, crushed with salt

2 medium sized tomatoes, grated (tinned ones will do well)

½ onion grated

freshly ground black pepper

1. Mash the avocados and add the rest of the ingredients.

2. Cover with clingfilm pressing it down onto the surface of the dip to stop discolouration.

3. Serve the avocado dip with toasted pitta bread, cut into wedges.

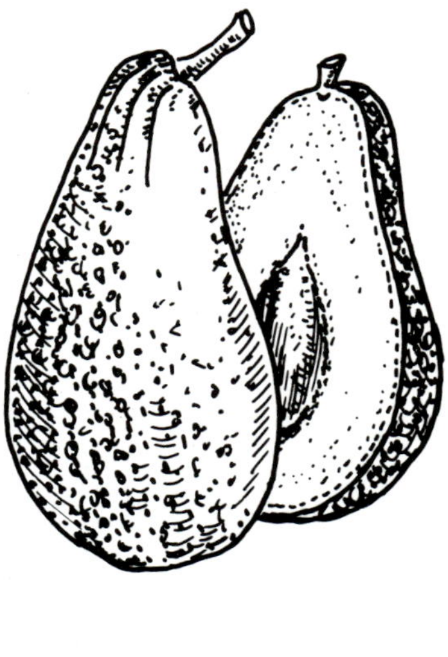

• A Cypriot Christmas Cake •

According to the Greek Orthodox religion Christmas is not an important feast, but western habits have worn off in Cyprus and year by year Christmas becomes more commercial.

British Christmas cake is certainly made by the Cypriots but in a slightly adapted form. Using local ingredients and adjusting the flavour of the cake to suit their tastes the Cypriots make their Christmas cake rich in almonds but low in butter. It is also paler in colour and much lighter in texture than ours, so not quite so rich. Orange flower water is sprinkled over the cooked cake instead of brandy just to add a fragrance particularly pertinent to the Middle East. Marzipan is the traditional covering for Cypriot Christmas cakes, they don't usually make up a white icing . . . but by that stage, it's up to you.

Ingredients

8oz (225g) butter or ½ tin spry pure vegetable shortening
2 glasses/8oz caster sugar
6 eggs, separated
4 tablespoons brandy
1 tablespoon rum
6oz (175g) currants
1lb (500g) sweetened fruit (either crystalised, glyko, fruit in thick syrup or candied fruit will do e.g. steam ginger, cherries, citrus peel, pineapple, angelica, even dried fruit that has been reconstituted in a sweet syrup
4oz (100g) walnuts, chopped
8oz (225g) almonds, ground with their skins on
grated rind of one lemon
1lb (½ kg) self raising flour
4 teaspoons baking powder

1. Beat the butter and sugar until light and fluffy.

2. Add the egg yolks, one at a time alternately with the alcohol.

3. In a separate bowl mix the currants, fruit, nuts, lemon rind, flour and baking powder.

4. Combine the two mixtures together and gently fold in the stiffly whisked egg whites.

5. Prepare a large 10″ diameter or about 30″ circumference (Cypriot measure) cake tin with a double layer of greaseproof paper on the bottom and around the sides.

6. Bake the cake in a moderate oven Gas 3-4 for about 1¾ hours. Cover the top with extra greaseproof paper if it becomes too brown. Test the cake with a metal skewer — if it comes out clean then the cake is done.

7. Sprinkle orange flower water over the cooked cake before wrapping in foil to keep until Christmas.

8. Marzipan and ice as you wish.

• Glyko •

"Would you like a cup of coffee?" we say to visitors by way of good manners and natural hospitality. In Cyprus it is just the same, but with every cup of coffee goes the offer of a piece of glyko too.

Glyko is simply fresh fruit that has been soaked in syrup to preserve it throughout the year. Because it is so delicious though, Glyko is kept for guests and high days and holidays.

Truthfully, Glyko is not prepared so much these days mainly because it is a time consuming process, but also our tastes are veering away from such very sweet dishes. But I just love it!

Some of the fruits that are turned into glyko in Cyprus are apples, cherries, plums, seville oranges or just the skins, small aubergines, melon skin and best of all, green walnuts or **karidhi.** The small Karidhi are called Karithakia. A similar preserve, but flavoured with cardamom, is made in Iran, where it is called Morabaye Gerdu.

Glyko Karidhi — First find a walnut tree and pick the nuts very green and not yet full size, so that the inner shell is still soft. Test a nut by pricking it deeply in several places with a darning needle, paying particular attention to the long crease on one side; this indicates the join of the forming shell and is the part which hardens first. If there is no resistance, cut the nut in half to check again. You will see the thick outer green covering progressing to white. The actual nut meat should be apparent — if it is clean and gelatinous, then the nuts are ready for the preserving pan. If the nut meat is not visible try again in a few days.

Ingredients

4lbs (2k) green walnuts, about 50
4 tablespoons slake lime
6 glasses/1½ lbs granulated sugar
1½ glasses/300ml water
thinly peeled rind of 1 lemon
large piece cinnamon bark
3 cloves
2 tablespoons lemon juice
2 tablespoons honey

1. To avoid getting black hands from the iodine in the nuts I suggest you wear rubber gloves.

2. Peel walnuts thinly with a sharp knife, then put them in cold water.

3. Leave the nuts covered by cold water for 8 days, changing the water daily.

4. Put lime in a glass of water and stir to dissolve. When dissolved, add walnuts and sufficient cold water to cover. Stir, then leave for 4 hours. (The lime toughens the outer shell so that the nuts don't disintegrate).

5. Drain walnuts and rinse well under a cold running tap.

6. Place walnuts in a large saucepan and cover with cold water. Bring to the boil and simmer gently, uncovered until tender — about 1½ hours. Test with a needle.

7. Drain walnuts, then pierce each in several places so that syrup can penetrate.

8. Place walnuts in a clean pan in layers, sprinkling 1 glass of sugar over each layer. Pour on water and leave for 2 hours, so that sugar can dissolve slowly.

9. Put on to heat, adding lemon rind, cinnamon bark and cloves to pan. Heat gently, shaking pan contents to help dissolve remaining sugar crystals. When syrup begins to boil, add lemon juice and boil for 5 minutes. Remove from heat, cover and leave for 24 hours.

10. Add honey to pan contents and return to the boil. Simmer gently for 10 minutes without stirring. Skim when necessary.

11. When syrup is very thick, the consistency of runny honey, the preserve is ready. Remove lemon rind, cinnamon and cloves. Ladle into hot sterilized jars and leave until cold before sealing. Store in a cool dark corner.

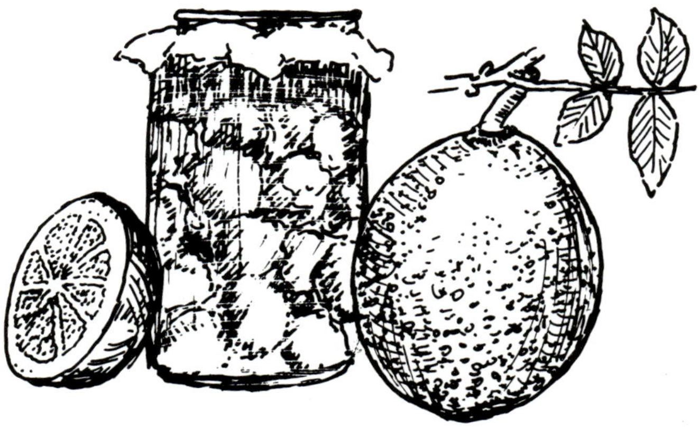

• Kourambiedhes — Shortbread •

Shortbread is made in so many parts of the world that it is hard to say where the recipe originated. These Greek shortbread biscuits have lots of chopped almonds in them which suits Cypriot cooking.

One thing that all these mouth watering 'melting' biscuits have in common is a delicate fragrance from rose water or orange flower water and a thick coat of icing sugar.

• Makes over 12 •

Ingredients

8oz (225g) butter (unsalted or lightly salted)
½ glass/2oz caster sugar
1 large egg yolk
1-2 tablespoons brandy
1 glass/4oz whole almonds
2 tablespoons cornflour
2½-3 glasses/10-12oz plain flour
orange flower water or rose water
icing sugar

1. Cream the butter, add the sugar, egg yolk and alcohol.

2. Blanch the almonds by pouring boiling water over them. Leave for 5 minutes to soften then drain the nuts and chop them coarsely, skins and all.

3. Add the almonds to the butter mixture and then work in the cornflour and enough plain flour to give a firm soft dough.

4. Break off small pieces the size of a large walnut. Shape into crescents, or roll into balls and flatten slightly with your hand.

5. Bake in a moderately slow oven gas 3-4, 325-350°F, 170-180°C for 20 minutes taking care not to let them brown. Leave on the tray for 10 minutes to cool.

6. Dip each cooked kourambiedhes into orange flower or rose water and then roll in icing sugar.

Kourambiedhes are even better if stored in a tin for a couple of days. This improves the flavour but tantalizes the hungry!

• Kouneli Stifado •

Kouneli is a cultivated rabbit, a very expensive ingredient in Cyprus. Lagos is what the Cypriots call a wild rabbit and this not only has a stronger and more agreeable flavour, but is free, if you have a huntsman for a friend.

Wednesday afternoon and Sunday morning is hunting time and more than 50% of the male population heads for the hills. Alas, they shoot almost anything that moves and some very small birds suffer at the guns of the hunters, but who would refuse the kind offer of a wild rabbit. Luckily, shooting periods and areas have now been restricted.

Stifado means onions! Whether you cook beef or rabbit, octopus or snails, make sure that you have lots of onions in the pot to sweeten the flavour of the casserole. Cinnamon is a spice often found in this Greek dish as well as bay leaves and red wine.

• Serves 4-6 •

Ingredients

3 tablespoons olive oil
1 medium sized rabbit, prepared and jointed
2 large cloves garlic, crushed
2 tablespoons wine vinegar
1 glass/8 tablespoons red wine
a stick of cinnamon
1 bay leaf
3 medium sized tomatoes, grated or 1½ tablespoons tomato puree
2 glasses/400ml hot water
salt and lots of freshly ground black pepper
8 tablespoons sunflower or vegetable oil
1½ (750g) pickling onions, peeled whole

1. Heat the oil in a large heavy based casserole and fry the rabbit joints to seal all sides.

2. Add the garlic, fry quickly then add the wine vinegar, wine, cinnamon, bay leaf, tomatoes, water and seasoning.

3. Cover and cook in a medium oven for about 45-50 minutes.

4. Meanwhile heat the sunflower oil in a large frying pan. Toss the onions in it gently for about 15 minutes until they are brown on all sides.

5. Add the browned onions to the stifado and continue to cook for a further 20 minutes.

6. The stifado should have a rich, thick sauce. If there is too much liquid left after the onions have been added (onions make extra juice) remove the lid and simmer the casserole over moderate heat to allow some of the juices to evaporate.

• Loukanika — Cypriot Sausages •

I shall first give the recipe for Loukanika given to me by a housewife from Pissouri village. The end result was superb, let me tell you, but I doubt that many of us have the time, dedication or application to follow her recipe though. It begins . . .

Start with 10 kilos of minced pork, of this 2½kg will be fat to make it soft and tasty, add 150gm salt, 1 coffee cut chinos (juniper) ½ crushed and ½ whole, 1 coffee cup dried crushed coriander seed, 1 coffee cup artichat (cumin) crushed, 1 coffee cup black pepper, ground but leave some whole.

. . . Mix all ingredients and cover with in dry red wine, stir each day, leave in a cool place for 6 days, adding more wine if necessary. On the 6th day, add more herbs and spices and fill the mixture into washed sausage skins. Hang the sausages up for 12 hours to dry. Smoke them twice a day for a week, suspended over a fire of aromatic woods, i.e. carob, juniper, spatcha and tyme, but don't use wood with sap such as pine.

After that either eat or keep the sausages in the fridge, and for long term storage keep them in a pot of rendered pig fat.

Now let me give a simpler recipe for an unsmoked loukanika, which really is worth a try.

• Serves 6 •

Ingredients

2lbs (1kg) boneless pork (with about 20% fat)

2 tablespoons fortified wine (madeira or port)

1 teaspoon whole black peppercorns

½ teaspoon ground black pepper

2 teaspoons ground coriander

¼ teaspoon ground cinnamon

¼ teaspoon whole cumin seeds

2 teaspoons salt

2 cloves of garlic

sausage casings (optional)

1. Chop or mince the pork coarsely.

2. In a glass or plastic bowl, combine the pork, wine and seasonings. Leave overnight in the fridge.

3. Soak the sausage skins in cold water for an hour to soften, then fill the meat mixture into them. (A funnel is handy for this).
Alternatively, roll the mixture into sausage shapes and toss in seasoned flour.

4. Store the sausages in the fridge until needed. Fry in a little fat over gentle heat or grill over charcoal.

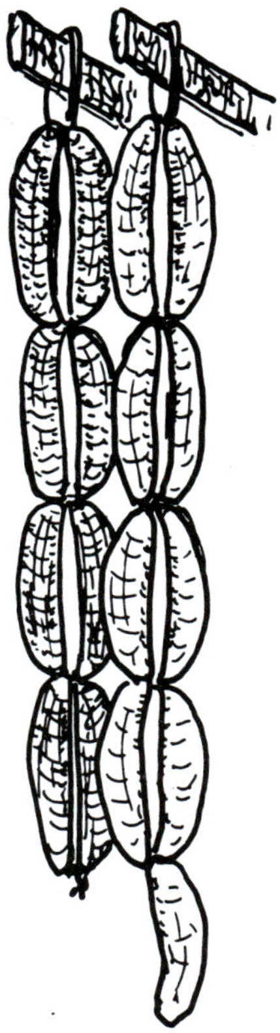

• Melomakarona — Honey Soaked Buns •

Christmas preparations don't really get under way until the last week, but then baking takes place with a vengeance. After the Christmas cake come the shortbreads and then these melomakarona. They are baked in huge quantities by every family in Cyprus and offered to visitors during the Christmas holiday.

Although the quanity of oil seems extravagent compared to British biscuits, it gives the melomakarona a pleasant soft texture.

• Makes over 12 •

Ingredients

4oz butter/1 glass Spry, melted

2 glasses/400ml sunflower oil

4 tablespoons caster sugar

grated rind of 2 oranges and 2 lemons

1 glass/200ml orange juice

juice of 1 lemon

2lbs (1k) plain flour

1 teaspoon baking powder

1½ teaspoon baking soda

Syrup

2 glasses caster sugar

1½ glasses of water

2 tablespoons honey

Coarsely ground almonds for decoration

First make the syrup.

Heat the sugar and water gently until dissolved, then boil for 10 minutes.

Add the honey and leave the syrup to cool.

1. Beat the butter, oil, sugar, fruit rinds and juice together.
2. Mix sifted flour with the baking powder and soda, add gradually to liquid mixture to make a light but firm dough.
3. Using your hands roll the dough into egg sized ovals and flatten onto a plain baking tin.
4. Using a fork make ridges along the top of the melomakarona.
5. Bake in a moderate oven Gas 4, 350°F, 180°C, for about 20 minutes.

Pour the cool syrup over the melomakarona as soon as they come out of the oven.

Sprinkle over coarsely ground almonds before serving.

• Moussaka •

"I was beginning to think that successive occupations (of Cyprus) had extirpated any trace whatsoever of the Greek genius when I was relieved by the sight of a bus with both back wheels missing, lying on its side against a house. It was just like home."

Lawrence Durrell from Bitter Lemons

How this passage reminds me of Cyprus, as does eating moussaka! Moussaka may have its roots in Greece but no-one makes individual moussakas in terracotta pots quite like the Cypriots.

• Serves 4-6 •

Ingredients

2lb (1k) aubergines or courgettes or a mixture of both (trimmed and sliced lengthways in thick slices)

2 large potatoes, cooked, pealed and sliced (optional)

½ glass/100ml olive or sunflower oil

2 medium onions, sliced

1lb (450g) minced beef or lamb

2 large tomatoes, grated or 1 x 400g tin of tomatoes

½ teaspoon ground cinnamon or 1 stick cinnamon

½ teaspoon rigani or dried oregano

½ glass/100ml red wine

salt and freshly ground black pepper

For the white sauce

3oz/75g butter

4 level tablespoons flour

1 pint warm milk

ground nutmeg

2 eggs

1 glass/2oz grated cheese – halloumi, kefalotiri or tasty cheddar

1. Immerse the aubergine slices in lightly salted water for 30 minutes, then rinse and squeezing them gently, pat dry with kitchen towel. The courgettes need no attention.

2. Fry the aubergine or courgette slices in ¾ of the oil, turning the slices so that they brown but don't cook through. Leave them to drain on kitchen paper.

3. In another pan fry the onions till soft in the rest of the oil then add the meat and stir to break it up. Add the tomatoes, herbs, spices, seasoning and wine and continue to cook for about 25 minutes when the liquid should have been absorbed.

4. For the white sauce, melt the butter in a saucepan, stir in the flour and then add the warm milk gradually, whisking hard to remove any lumps. Take the saucepan away from the heat and stir in the seasoning, spices and cheese. Make sure that the sauce has cooled before adding the eggs.

To assemble the moussaka

Either use a 10″ x 10″ (25cm x 25cm) baking dish or 6 individual pots and line the base with slices of cooked aubergine or courgette. (Add a layer of cooked potato if you are using it).

Now spread the meat in a layer over the aubergine and cover with the remainder of the aubergine and potato.

Cover the top of the moussaka with the white sauce and bake in a moderate oven Gas 4, 350°F for about 50 minutes until the top is a good crusty brown.

• Pasticcio •

Tasty and filling, this pasta dish is a combination of lasagne and macaroni cheese and masquerades under the title of Pastitso in Greece or Pasticcio here in Cyprus. It is very popular and forms part of any celebration meal, be it a wedding, christening or village festival.

I enjoyed my first pasticcio at the monastry of St. Neophytos just north of Paphos. The Abbot had invited a group of visitors to share his Sunday lunch, what a meal, lucky us!

The Cypriots like to cut their pasticcio into wedges rather like a moussaka. It suits my family better to be cooked with less macaroni and more sauce!

• This recipe will feed up to 10 people •

Ingredients

1lb (225g) thick macaroni
4oz (100g) butter
4oz (100g) grated strong cheddar or kefalotiri
pinch nutmeg
salt and pepper
3 eggs, lightly beaten

Meat Sauce

1½ lb /750g ground beef
1 large onion, chopped
1 clove garlic, crushed
2 tablespoons tomato paste
½ glass/100ml dry red or white wine
1 glass/200ml stock (approximately)
2 tablespoons chopped parsley
pinch of sugar
salt and pepper

Cream Sauce

3oz/75g butter
3 tablespoons/3oz plain flour
4 glasses/1½ pints milk
pinch of nutmeg
salt and pepper
2 eggs lightly beaten

1. Cook macaroni in plenty of boiling salted water until just tender. Drain and return to the warm pan.

2. Add the butter and stir to melt then leave to cool. Stir in half of the cheese, seasonings and eggs.

3. *Make meat sauce.* Dry fry the ground beef until the fat runs and the mince begins to brown. Add the onion and garlic and cook till soft. Add remaining meat sauce ingredients, cover and simmer over gentle heat for 20 minutes.

4. *Make cream sauce.* Melt butter in a saucepan, stir in flour and cook gently for 2 minutes. Add all the milk, bring sauce to the boil, whisking hard with a metal whisk. Boil gently for 1 minute then cool. Add the eggs and seasoning.

5. *To assemble pasticcio* - Butter a large casserole dish. Spoon half of the cooked macaroni evenly over the base. Cover with the meat sauce and fill the dish with the remaining macaroni. Pour over the cream sauce, sprinkle remaining cheese on top and cook in a moderate oven for about 50 minutes until golden brown.

• Mouchentra — Green Lentil and Rice Pilaf •

Mouchentra or Moujendra in Cyprus, Mujadara in Syria and Megadarra in Lebanon. This dish of lentils and rice is supposedly the original 'potage of lentils' for which Esau sold his birthright.

Eleftheria, a friend from Nicosia, remembers eating this at the American University in Beirut. It was served every Friday evening, with a sort of kebab and taboulleh.

I first ate Moutchentra here in Cyprus at a small family run spa hotel in the hills above Paphos. It was served with chunks of roast lamb and roast potatoes, and its mildness of flavour was perfect foil for the richness of the meal.

Allow about half an hour to prepare Moutchentra and serve it on its own, with a bowl of plain yogurt or with practically any main course.

• Serves 4 •

Ingredients

1 glass/6oz green or brown lentils
1 glass/6 oz long grain rice
1 large onion, sliced thinly
3 tablespoons olive oil
lemon juice to taste
salt
pepper

1. Pick over the lentils and wash them well.

2. Boil gently in about a pint of water for 10 to 15 minutes, or until almost cooked but not quite.

3. Add the rice, bring the pan back to the boil then turn the heat down.

4. Simmer for about 15 to 20 minutes, until the rice is tender, adding more water if the liquid is absorbed too quickly. The mouchentra should begin to look quite mushy.

5. Fry the sliced onion in a little olive oil until it begins to colour. Stir this into the cooked rice and lentils together with the olive oil, lemon juice and seasoning.

• Pourgouri Pilafi — Cracked Wheat Pilaf •

The Arabs call it burghul, to a Cypriot it must be pourgouri — what is it? — cracked wheat of course!

Prepared from hulled wheat, the grain is steamed until partly cooked then dried before being ground. Pourgouri is available in fine and coarse grades.

Since the Turks ruled the eastern Mediterranean during the Ottoman Empire, pourgouri has been a vital part of the Levantine diet. Eaten more often than rice and pasta, cracked wheat is an ingredient found in every Cypriot store cupboard.

This may not appear to be a very splendid dish, but its star-rating qualities are in its simplicity. Always serve pourgouri pilafi with some wedges of lemon and lots of thick natural yogurt . . . wonderful!

• Serves 4-6 •

Ingredients

2 tablespoons olive oil
1 medium onion, finely sliced
1oz (25g) vermicelli
8oz (225g) pourgouri or bulgar (cracked wheat)
1½ glasses/300ml chicken stock
salt and black pepper
2 medium tomatoes, peeled and sliced

1. Heat the oil in a heavy based casserole and saute the onion and tomato for a couple of minutes until it softens but doesn't brown.

2. Stir in the vermicelli, breaking it with your hands. Continue to fry with the onion for a couple of minutes until it begins to absorb the oil.

3. Rinse the pourgouri under the cold tap, then add to the casserole.

4. Add the stock and seasoning. Cover and simmer gently for 8-10 minutes or until all the stock is absorbed.

5. Leave the pilafi to sit for five minutes before serving. Fork through at the last minute.

• Garides Me Fetta — Prawns with Fetta Cheese •

"Everyone pulls the quilt over to his side"

A Greek proverb.

Perhaps this proverb is taking a dig at me, for I know that this recipe really belongs in the Greek cuisine, but I had to include it with Cyprus recipes because it is so good. Fresh prawns don't find their way to Cyprus very often but I sometimes make this dish with large frozen ones and we all enjoy it just the same.

Ingredients

4 large ripe tomatoes

8oz (225g) cooked prawns (boil or simmer fresh prawns, leave frozen prawns as they are)

5 tablespoons olive oil

1 large onion, finely chopped

6 tablespoons dry white wine

1½ tablespoons finely chopped parsley

4oz (100g) fetta cheese, cut into cubes

a pinch of salt

freshly ground black pepper

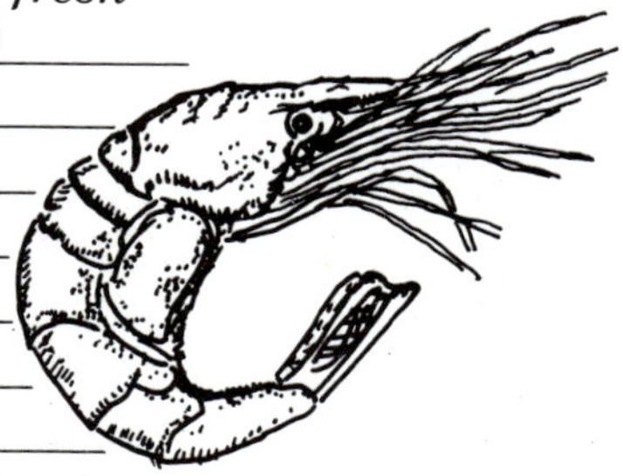

1. Pour boiling water over the tomatoes, count slowly to 10 then drain and run the tomatoes under the cold tap. Peel with a small sharp knife and cut into quarters. Squeeze out the seeds and discard. Chop the flesh.

2. Heat the oil in a large, heavy frying pan over moderate heat.

3. Add the onions and cook gently for about 5 minutes, until soft but not brown.

4. Stir in the tomatoes, wine, 1 tablespoon of the parsley, salt and some pepper. Bring to the boil and cook briskly, uncovered, until the mixture thickens to a light puree.

5. Add the prawns and cook for 2 minutes.

6. Stir in the cheese, taste for seasoning and sprinkle with the rest of the parsley.

7. Serve directly from the frying pan with a crusty loaf of bread.

• Psari Sto Fourno — Fish Baked in the Oven •

This Cypriot method of baking fish is simple and successful.

The addition of potatoes with the fish adds to the taste.

Psari Sto Fourno is rarely served in tavernas due to its preparation and cooking time but Cypriot families would be proud to cook it at home for you.

• Serves 4 •

Ingredients

- *1 large fish or two of medium size, weighing about 3 lbs (1½ kg)*
- *juice of 1 lemon*
- *salt*
- *freshly ground black pepper*
- *4 tablespoons olive oil*
- *2 large potatoes peeled and sliced*
- *3 cloves of garlic, crushed*
- *3 tablespoons finely chopped parsley*
- *3 large tomatoes, peeled and sliced*
- *2 sticks celery, chopped*
- *2 carrots, peeled and diced*

1. Clean and scale fish if necessary. Wipe dry and season inside and out with lemon juice, salt and pepper. Cover and refrigerate for 1-2 hours.

2. Oil a large baking dish. Spread the potato slices over the base. Add the garlic and most of the parsley.

3. Put the fish in the dish and pour over a little of the oil. Lay the tomatoes on top of the fish and arrange the celery and carrots around the sides of the dish. Season well and add remaining oil.

4. Bake in a moderate oven for 35-40 minutes, covering the dish for the first 15 minutes.

5. Serve fish once the flesh flakes easily and the vegetables are cooked. Sprinkle with remaining parsley.

• Rizogalo — Rice Pudding •

Greek rice pudding is quite unlike the English variety: it is thicker and creamier, and can be very good indeed.

Mastic, the strange resinous gum of a species of pine which grows in the Paphos region, often flavours the rizogalo in Cyprus. Cypriot children in particular enjoy Mastic because they are given it as chewing gum since it is thought to strengthen the teeth.

Ground allspice is a good alternative to mastic.

Ingredients

2 tablespoons short grain or pudding rice
½ glass/100ml water
1 pint/600ml milk
3 tablespoons sugar
2 teaspoons cornflour
1 egg yolk
2 teaspoons rose water
1 pellet mastic, crushed
or ½ teaspoon ground allspice

1. Wash the rice and soak in the water.

2. Bring 1 pint milk to the boil with the sugar then stir in the rice and water. Bring back to the boil and simmer steadily for 40 minutes, covered, until most of the milk, but not all, has been absorbed.

3. Blend the cornflour with a tablespoon of water and add to the rice, cooking for a further 5 minutes, stirring constantly. Add the mastic now too.

4. Beat the egg yolk with a tablespoon of cold milk and stir into the rice, take the pan off the heat immediately and stir well.

5. Add the rose water and serve the rice pudding cold with a sprinkling of allspice over each bowl.

• Vodhino Stifado — Rich Beef Stew with Onions •

A Greek dish, Stifado is served at almost every taverna in Cyprus. Tender chunks of beef in a rich tomato sauce, sweetened by a mass of cooked onions and spiced with a subtle hint of vinegar; stifado is the very heart of Cypriot cuisine.

Beef is a rare commodity throughout the Middle East and is greatly appreciated in Cyprus.

Vinegar was used to help preserve a dish as well as tenderise in the past, while today it has new fame as a vital ingredient to enhance sauces just before serving.

• Serves 4-6 •

Ingredients

2lb (1kg) braising or stewing beef, cut into largish chunks
2lb (1kg) pickling or very small onions, peeled
3-4 tablespoons oil
2 cloves garlic
2 tablespoons wine vinegar
6 ripe tomatoes, grated or 1 tablespoon tomato puree
2 bay leaves
1 stick of cinnamon
1 glass/200ml red wine or water
1 teaspoon sugar (optional)
salt and pepper

1. Heat the oil in a large heavy based casserole. Fry the onions until brown on all sides, remove.
2. Fry the meat, a few chunks at a time to seal.
3. Replace all the meat in the casserole, add the garlic and vinegar. Let it boil up well for a minute.
4. Add the tomatoes, bay leaves, cinnamon, seasonings and enough wine or water to just cover the meat.
5. Cover and cook the stifado very gently for about 2 hours.
6. Replace the onions, add more liquid if necessary and cook for a further ½ hour.
7. Towards the end of cooking it may be necessary to remove the lid and cook the stifado briskly to reduce the sauce, which should be rich and thick.
8. Chips or roast potatoes would accompany a stifado in Cyprus. I prefer to serve jacket or creamy mashed potatoes with mine.

• Tavas Arni — Lamb Tavas •

This dish is named after the pot in which it is cooked. A tava is made of unglazed terracotta with a snug-fitting lid. Before the advent of ovens the tava was placed on glowing embers in a hole in the ground with earth packed around and on top of the pot. In Cyprus, they say that the best tava is still made in a *fourno* or clay oven.

A Cypriot tava pot may not be easy to find but there are many terracotta pots on the market now, just look for one with a well fitting lid.

Don't wash your tava pot in soap, just wipe clean, rinse with hot water and leave to dry.

The characteristic flavour of the dish comes from 'artisha' or cumin seed which is grown in great profusion on the island. The amount in the recipe may be rather overpowering, so adjust to your taste.

• Serves 4-6 •

Ingredients

1½ lb (675g) boneless lamb, shoulder or leg
2 tablespoons olive or vegetable oil
2 large onions, diced
3 large tomatoes, skinned and chopped
2 medium potatoes, cubed same size as meat (optional)
2 teaspoons cumin, freshly ground
salt
black pepper, freshly ground
water to moisten

1. Cut the lamb into 1¼″ (3cm) cubes. Place in the bottom of a not too big casserole or tava pot with the oil.

2. Add onions, tomatoes, potatoes, cumin and seasoning. Pour in enough water to moisten but not to cover the meat completely. Stir well.

3. Cover tightly and cook in a slow oven 300°F, Gas 2, 150°C for 2-2½ hours, or until lamb is tender.

A cast iron casserole will produce a lot of juices with a tava, so I suggest serving chunks of fresh bread to soak them up.

• Trahanas — Pourgouri and Yogurt Soup •

This thick nourishing winter soup can be found in many of the Middle Eastern countries. It is eaten also in Lebanon and Syria and to a lesser extent in Iran where it is called Kashk.

Trahanas is made from cracked wheat or pourgouri which is mixed with milk or yogurt and left to ferment, this gives it a sharp tangy flavour. After fermentation it is salted, spread on a cloth to dry, then cut into chunks and stored away for winter.

When trahanas are cooked with water they make a nourishing breakfast for hard working labourers, but trahanas are usually cooked in stock and served as a filling supper soup.

I have adapted the basic recipe for trahanas so that it can be made without the dried trahana pieces, which are only available in Cypriot shops. The flavour may differ slightly but the main combination of wheat and sharp yogurt is still there.

• Serves 4 •

Ingredients

2 pints well flavoured chicken stock

8-10 pieces of trahana

or 4 tablespoons pourgouri and 1 small tub natural yogurt

fresh lemon juice

salt and freshly ground black pepper

1. In a large saucepan heat the stock and add the trahana or pourgouri. Simmer until tender, about 15 minutes.

2. Stir the yogurt into the cracked wheat if you didn't use trahana pieces.

3. Add enough lemon juice to bring out the flavour of the soup and season to taste with salt and pepper.

4. Serve your trahanas hot, just as it is or with a little finely chopped tomato for added colour and some cubes of halloumi to vary the texture.

• Vasilopitta — New Year's Cake •

Rather like our Christmas pudding the Vasilopitta has treasure hidden in it.

This is the cake made for St. Basil who celebrates his Saints day on New Years eve. Cypriot families lay a table in His honour in the hope that St. Basil will bring good luck and fortune in the forthcoming year.

The Vasilopitta is cut a few hours after the end of the past year, or on New Year's morning. The first slice is cut for Christ, the second for the house, the third for the poor and the rest is distributed between the family. The person who finds the hidden coin will have luck for the year.

Ingredients

12oz (375g) plain flour
3oz (75g) butter
4 tablespoons vegetable, sunflower or groundnut oil
4oz (100g) sugar
¾ glass/150ml fresh orange juice
2 tablespoons brandy
2 teaspoons baking powder
1 tablespoon grated orange rind
4 eggs

1. Beat the butter in a big bowl until soft then add egg yolks, sugar, oil and orange rind.

2. Gradually add the brandy and orange juice.

3. Lastly fold in the flour, baking powder and whisked egg white.

4. Pour the mixture into a lined and buttered tin and cook in a medium oven Gas 4, 350°F, 180°C.

5. Cover the top of the cake with thick paper if it turns brown before the cake is cooked in the middle.

N.B. Don't forget to sink a coin into the cake when it's cooked!

• Yiouvetsi — Lamb Casserole with Pasta •

"The driver was doing one of those laughing and shrugging acts which drive travellers out of their minds all over the Levant"

Lawrence Durrel from Bitter Lemons

This dish of casseroled lamb with tiny rice shaped pieces of pasta is as Cypriot as the quote above, but hardly likely to stir anyone except in pleasurable appreciation.

• Serves 4-6 •

Ingredients

6 thick lamb chops

2 tablespoons sunflower or olive oil

1 large onion, finely chopped

2 tablespoons tomato puree

1 glass/200ml chopped, peeled tomatoes

3 cloves

large piece cinnamon bark

salt

freshly ground black pepper

about 1½ pints/4-5 glasses boiling water or stock

6oz/2 glasses kritharaki (rice shaped pasta) or small pasta twists or shells

2 tablespoons grated kefalotiri or parmesan cheese

4 tablespoons diced halloumi or feta cheese

1. Put lamb chops in a large baking dish, pour over the oil and bake in a hot oven for 15 minutes.

2. Lower the oven temperature to moderate and add onion. Cook for another 10 minutes.

3. Add tomato puree, chopped tomatoes, cloves, cinnamon and seasoning. Baste meat with liquid, cover and cook for a further half hour until meat is tender, adding a little of the water or stock if necessary.

4. When lamb is cooked add remaining stock or water and stir in pasta. Cook in the oven or on top for 20 minutes, stirring occasionally, and add more liquid if necessary.

5. When pasta is tender, sprinkle cheese over and return to oven for 5 minutes. Serve immediately.

Cyprus Sherry
Commandaria
White CYPRUS WINE
RED CYPRUS WINE
FULLY BODDIED
OUZO
CYPRUS BRANDY

SHOPPING FOR CYPRIOT INGREDIENTS

I hope you are tempted to try some of the recipes in this book. However, I do appreciate how frustrating it is not to be able to find the right ingredients. So I suggest that you take my advice and follow this plan . . .

First visit your nearest Cypriot or Greek restaurant to taste their menu. If you like it then speak to the cook and ask him where he collects his various ingredients.

Failing this, check through the yellow pages for Cypriot delicatessens or green grocers. Now buzz along there and lean on their infallable good nature to tell you where the best Cypriot suppliers are to be found.

Supermarkets, the larger the better, are probably best stocked for ingredients such as

Feta cheese
Halloumi cheese
Anari or ricotta cheese
Cracked wheat or pourgouri
Chickpeas
Pitta bread
Filo pastry
Pickled vineleaves
Coriander seeds
Taramasalata
Hummus
Olives

Ask your local chemist for

Rose Water and Orange Flower Water

The fishmonger should provide

Octopus, Squid, Cuttlefish, Red Mullet and Sea Bream *to say nothing of* ***Sword Fish.***

The off licence will help with

Pomegranite juice or Grenadine, Ouzo

Cyprus red and white wines are plentiful and their list long. Popular brands include:

Amathus, Keo Hock, Arsinoe, Kolossi, Palomino, White Lady, Amorosa, Aphrodite, Bellapais, Thisbe, St. Hilarion, Hirondelle, St. Panteleimon, Kykko, Olympus, Salamis, Afames, Othello, Amathus, Laona, Laona Nouveau *and of course the most famous Cyprus wine of all* ***Commandaria.***

DID YOU KNOW THAT Cyprus exports fresh items to Britain such as . . .

Grapefruit, Lemons, Oranges, Tangerines, Apricots, Avodados, Grapes, Cherries, Strawberries and Melons.

As well as . . .

Artichokes, Asparagus, Aubergines, Beans, Carrots, Beetroot, Capsicum, Celery, Chillies, Chinese leaves, Coriander, Courgettes, Cucumber, Endive, Indian Vegetables, Kohlrabi, Leeks, Lettuce, Parsley, Potatoes, Pumpkin, Radish, Okra, Spring Onions, Spinach and of juicy Mediterranean Tomatoes.

FAILING ALL THIS ADVICE, if you still can't find the local Cypriot flavour in your neighbourhood, then I suggest you contact your nearest ***CYPRUS INFORMATION CENTRE AND TRADE OFFICE.***

UNITED KINGDOM
211/213 Regent Street
London W1R 8DA
Tel. 071-734 4791/2

BELGIUM
83 Rue de la Loi
Lex Building, 4th Floor
1040 Brussels
Tel. 2301295

GERMANY
16 Pipinstrasse
5000 Cologne 1
Tel. 235160/69

GREECE
36 Voukourestiou Street
Athens
Tel. 3646320 or 3646420

USA
13b 40th Street
New York, NY 100016
Tel. (212) 2139100

CZECHOSLOVAKIA
Dubecska Street 36/1228
Prague 2
Tel. 256376

JAPAN
Palais France Building
6-1 Jingumae 1-Chome
Shibuya-Ku
Tokyo 150
Tel. 03-497 9329

KUWAIT
Abdullah Mubarak St.
Al Mogil Centre
9th Floor
PO Box 22034, Safat
Tel. 2433075

UNITED ARAB EMIRATES
Flat No. 11,
First Floor
Juma Al Majid Bldg
(Old DNATA)
Jamal Abdul Nasser Sq.
Deira Dubai
Tel. 282411 or 282994

A BRIEF HISTORY OF CYPRUS

To understand contemporary Cypriot food it might be wise to glance back into the history of this much troubled island.

Geographically, Cyprus lies at the eastern end of the mediterranean. Asia Minor and Syria can be seen from it with the naked eye, and Beirut, Haifa, Port Said, Alexandria and Rhodes are within the sailor's or flier's easy reach.

The third largest Island in the Mediterranean, it covers approximately 3,572 sq. miles or 9,250 sq. kms. The north coast of the island is roughly 45 miles from the Turkish coast. From the extreme eastern points of the island to Syria it is less than sixty miles, and on clear days from certain heights, such as Stavrovouni, its shores are discernible. Both mountain ranges (Troodos and Pentadaktylos) are particularly impressive.

The finest springs in the island originate from the southern flank of Pentadaktylos, appearing at Kythrea. Their waters in more anient times, by means of an aqueduct, supplied the needs of Salamis, some twenty three miles away.

The central plain lying between the mountain ranges is called the Mesaoria and makes a safe location for the capital city of Nicosia. The name of the island may well have come from the copper which in antiquity, long before the Roman period, was exported from the island. Silver was also mined in ancient Cyprus.

More than thirty sites can be attributed to the Neolithic or Chalcolithic periods.

Greeks were already settled in great numbers on the island by the end of the 13th century BC. So it seems that the Greek colonisation of Cyprus began after the fall of Troy and since then Cyprus and Greece have been intricately linked.

Some would say that the Cypriots are not pure Greeks for the influences and invading powers which have beset Cyprus over the past three thousand years have all added to the Cypriot character. Of the early visitors to Cyprus the Phoenicians (commercial traders) were made welcome before the arrival of the Persians.

The rising Greek influence is seen in the fact that for the first time in Cyprus the Greek alphabet appears on the coins.

Cyprus had immeasurable wealth and in 58 BC Rome seized the island and plundered it ruthlessly. This was the last stage in the encirclement of Egypt, following logically on the acquisition of Colicia, Cyrene and Syria.

Under the Romans Cyprus flourished and gymnasia, theatres and libraries were established.

Christianity came to Cyprus in 45-46 AD when Paul and Barnabas, attended by John Mark set out from Antioch on their historic mission. From Seleucia they crossed to Salamis, the native city of Barnabas, and preached in the Jewish synagogues there. They travelled through the whole island of Cyprus to Paphos where Paul performed a miracle to proconsul Sergius Paulus who was converted to Christianity. (He temporarily blinded a member of the court).

The earliest monastic foundations in Cyprus go back to the fourth century. St. Helena gave her relics of the crucifixion to the monastery of the Holy Cross on Stavrovouni which had been established by the Basilican Order. She found the island full of snakes so on a second visit filled the boats with cats.

Two monks smuggled silkworms to Cyprus from the Far East and the silk industry became, but is no longer, one of the most important on the island.

Peace in Cyprus was to come to an abrupt end when, from the 7th to the 10th centuries the Arab raids brought great destruction. On 10th April 1191 Richard the Lionheart, on his way to the third crusade in the Holy land sailed into Limassol harbour. He broke his journey in order to search for his missing ships including that which carried his bride Berengaria and his sister Joan which escaped a storm and was lying off the Cyprus coast. After a somewhat cool reception from the ruler Isaac, who ill-treated his surviving troops from the storm, Richard seized control of the island, much to the joy of the islanders who suffered from the tyrannous ruler.

Owning Cyprus was no easy task for crusader Richard so he sold it to the Knights Templar. They proved to be unfair rulers. In 1192 Cyprus was taken over (bought) by Guy de Lusignan who established a dynasty with a long future and so began the Frankish period.

From the Byzantium Empire to the Turkish Conquest, Cyprus came under a succession of Latin rulers. First the French (Franks) then the Geneoese (only Famagusta 1374-1464), followed by the Venetians.

This proved to be a time of prosperity for Cyprus but during the whole of the Latin occupation, there was never anything but conflict between the Latin and Catholic churches.

There was still a great deal of piracy at the eastern end of the Mediterranean and many earthquakes as well as plagues and recurring droughts to say nothing of the locusts which devastated the countryside on a regular basis.

The Cypriots suffered under the hands of invading Arabs in the 15th century. They attacked from the south coast of the island spreading fear and terror as they slaughtered huge numbers of islanders and captured a considerable number which were taken to Egypt.

The Lusignans ruled the island on a feudal system. Ecclesiastically their policy was to effect the subordination of the Greek Orthodox church to their Latin church. Yet the period 1192-1489 was the most brilliant epoch of Cyprus' varied history.

With the Venetians as the ruling power (1489-1571), however, there was a greater mingling between the classes. Old Cypriote and Frankish blood mixed with foreign elements, mainly Spanish and Italian.

In 1517 Sultan Selim I attacked and defeated the Mameluke dynasty in Egypt, this marked the beginning of the Ottoman Empire. Syria was taken in 1516, Rhodes in 1522. The capture of Constantinople in 1453 signalled the end of the Byzantine Empire, sent 'cold shivers' across Christian Europe. Cyprus lived in fear of the Turks and war seemed imminent for decades. Kyernia (Kyrenia), Famagusta and Nicosia were fortified although the Venetians had dismantled St Hilarion, Buffavento and Kantara to cut the maintenance costs. Paphos at this time was in ruins with few inhabitants and Lemessos (Limassol) had a good tower but a destroyed castle.

Despite his threats, Suleiman didn't attack Cyprus but his successor, Selim II was determined to conquer the island, (some said for his love of Cypriot sweet wine). Venetian hopes that all Christian denominations would rally to the aid of Cyprus against the moslem Turks were ill-founded and the first aggressors landed in 1570.

The number of dead on the first day was said to be estimated in thousands, and as with the capture of any other Christian city by the Turks, there was general savagery throughout the island.

As for religion, one might think that by having Moslem leaders the Cypriots were now under the worst possible threat to their Greek Orthodox religion. But not so for the Turks allowed the Greeks to maintain their religious beliefs and actually endowed the church with certain political powers, such as the collecting of taxes. This power grew as the Turkish dominance wained and with the influx of many Greek mainlanders. Cypriot children were also given a Greek dominated education by the church-run schools.

Looking back to the Byzantium Empire, we see that the Orthodox Church was, even then, given ecclesiastical independence. The Archbishop was granted three privileges by Zeno the Byzantine Emperor; He was allowed to wear a purple cloak at church festivals, to carry an imperial sceptre instead of a pastoral staff and to sign in red ink. In 1260 the Greek Orthodox Church again showed its strength when Pope Alexander IV ordered the Greek bishops to come under the authority of the Latin Archbishops. The Cypriots began a united fight against the oppressor, foreign rule and foreign church. This hatred charged a spirit of resistance which contributed to the birth of Cypriot nationalism. The battle between the Catholics from Rome and the Greek Orthodox finally ended with the Turkish invasion when the muslim Turks simply restored the predominance of the Church of the Greek masses.

Following in the wake of Ottoman conquest, Cyprus suffered desolation. The Turks, who never learnt Greek, had little means of communication, even though they numbered one in five of the population compared to the Greek Christians. Their existence in Cyprus was uneasy, always suspecting that there was an eminent attack especially in 1769 when the Ottoman Empire was at war with Russia. After the defeat of the Turkish fleet off Chios the Russians had complete command of the eastern Mediterranean. Seeing Russia as the protector of the Orthodox faith, the Greek Cypriot bishops showed their support for the Russian interests against the French and Catholicism.

Next came the Greek War of Independence and Greek Cyprus felt its right to the aspirations in Greece. The Moslems, however, to safeguard the interests of Turkey performed an ugly mass massacre of the Christians. Emigration from Cyprus went on vigorously during these years. The Cypriots went for the most part to Greece, but also elsewhere; Trieste, Venice, Leghorn, Marseilles and Egypt which offered them economic autonomy. It is estimated that some 20,000—25,000 escaped over ten years. In Greece they obtained Greek citizenship and soon afterwards returned to Cyprus, no longer Rayahs of the Moslem state but Greek citizens.

It was at Larnaca that the first British troops, under Vice-Admiral Lord John Hay, disembarked on 4 July 1878 to take possession of the island in the name of Queen Victoria and it was here in Larnaca that the British flag was hoisted for the first time.

The general feeling of both Greeks and Turks appeared to be one of welcome for the new dispensation and hope for the future. The bishop of Kition, Kyprianos, read an address of welcome *"We accept the change of government inasmuch as we trust that Great Britain will help Cyprus, as it did the Ionian islands, to be united with mother Greece, with which it is naturally connected."*

So began the fiercest fight by the Greek Cypriots for unity with Greece, for Enosis was re-born.

After the annexation of Cyprus to the British Crown in 1914, a royal commission was demanded by the Greek Cypriots from the British Government, but refused.

Recent history of Cyprus tells how British resistance to the Greek Cypriot demands for enosis with Greece caused much public disorder on the island. Finally the Eoka guerilla campaign forced the British to the bargaining table and the Zürich-London agreement of 1959, finally set up the Cyprus Republic in 1960.

Enosis, though, has taken a back seat since 1974 when Turkey invaded Cyprus and now occupies the northern part of the island which they call the Turkish Republic.

Nothing could have caused more heartache to a Greek Cypriot than to have his precious island divided, and the government of today is working endlessly for the cause of re-unification.

Let's hope that this latest problem, for the sake of the Island and its people, will be solved in the not too distant future.

It must be seen as significant, though, that after 8,000 years of history Cyprus is still a troubled country. How many invasions and dominating ruling powers have the Cypriots survived?

What of the Cypriot character that emerges out of all this strife?

Bloody minded, no, determined and stoic, definitely.

Most of all, Cypriots bear few grudges, accept fate and live from day to day with optimism.

INDEX

COLOUR PHOTOS

INTERWORLD'S OTHER CYPRUS PUBLICATIONS

- **THE MAKING OF MODERN CYPRUS**
  Dr. S. Panteli ISBN 0 948853 09 3
- **APHRODITE CYPRIS — The Mythology of Cyprus**
  Stass Paraskos ISBN 0 948853 05 0
- **CYPRUS IN PICTURES**
  ISBN 0 948853 01 8
- **EXPLORE CYPRUS**
  ISBN 0 948853 15 8
- **PAPHOS — Land of Aphrodite**
  Renos Lavithis ISBN 0 948853 14 X